PAPUA NEW GUINEA

Science

Grade 7

Student Book

Kenneth Rouse

OXFORD

Oxford University Press is a department of the University of Oxford. It furthers the University's objective of excellence in research, scholarship, and education by publishing worldwide. Oxford is a registered trademark of Oxford University Press in the UK and in certain other countries.

Published in Australia by
Oxford University Press
Level 8, 737 Bourke Street, Docklands, Victoria 3008, Australia

First published 2008
Reprinted 2008 (twice), 2009, 2011, 2013, 2014 (twice), 2016, 2017, 2018, 2021, 2023, 2025

ISBN 978 0 19 555516 5

Typeset by Pier Vido
Illustrated by Uramina and Nelson Ltd
Printed in China by Golden Cup Printing Co. Ltd

Oxford University Press Australia & New Zealand is committed to sourcing paper responsibly.

Acknowledgments
The author and publisher wish to thank the following copyright holders for granting permission to reproduce their material. Sources are as follows:
Photolibrary/SPL/Alexis Rosenfeld p. 20 (left); Photolibrary/Gillianne Tedder Photography p. 70; Photolibrary/SPL/Dr M.A. Ansary p. 75 (top right); Photolibrary/SPL/Andrew Lambert Photography p. 76; Photo courtesy of Mark O'Brien p. 82 (left); Photolibrary/Imagestate Ltd p. 82 (right); Photolibrary/SPL/J.C. Revy p. 110 (left); Photolibrary/SPL/Fredrick Fransson p. 111 (top left); Photo courtesy of the South Tyrol Museum of Archaeology p. 118 (right); Photolibrary/SPL/Ronald Royer p. 124 (left).
Every effort has been made to trace the original source of copyright material contained in this book. The publisher would be pleased to hear from copyright holders to rectify any errors or omissions.

Contents

Working scientifically

Chapter summary

In this chapter you will have an opportunity to:

- find out about ways of doing investigations that are fair
- use simple equipment to gather information and present what you have found out
- present your conclusions based on the information that you have collected and what you have learned from your experience
- decide if a test that you have designed and carried out is fair
- find out how science can be used to improve everyday life and the responsibility related to those choices.

Syllabus references

Strand: Working scientifically

Sub-strand: Working scientifically

Outcomes: 7.1.1 Critically question their understandings of the broader environment and learn to make informed decisions based on scientific methods

Key facts

- People are interested in the things they find around them and often want to find out more about why things happen and how they work.
- When we want to find out about something and understand it better, we often carry out experiments or investigations.
- Investigations often start with a question or a problem. We choose a method in order to get some results and then we make a conclusion. This way of doing things is called the scientific method.
- When we are planning an investigation we must make sure that it is fair. Then we can find out why things happen and how they work.
- We often have to make and use simple equipment to collect information that will help us to carry out investigations.
- When we have collected information we can use it to make and support a conclusion.
- After carrying out an investigation we should decide if it was a fair test.
- Science can be used to improve community life, but the choices that we make must be responsible choices that are based on reliable information.

The meaning of science

Science can mean different things in different situations. For example, science can help us to find out how nature works, how the world works and how the **universe** works. However, science is more than learning about the world. Science is also a way of

- doing things
- looking at things
- thinking about things.

Finding out about our surroundings

Most people are interested in the things that are happening in their environment and try to understand why these things happen. We usually start to find out about our surroundings from the time we are very young. We know that babies and small children like to touch, taste, squeeze, throw and drop things. In this way they learn the rules that make things behave in the way they do. When small children play they are doing little experiments and finding out about the world around them. For example, small children might find out about the difference between food and other objects by putting them in their mouth. Some of the little experiments that children do might give them results that they do not expect and might even be dangerous. Parents, aunties and uncles usually protect children from hurting themselves in this way.

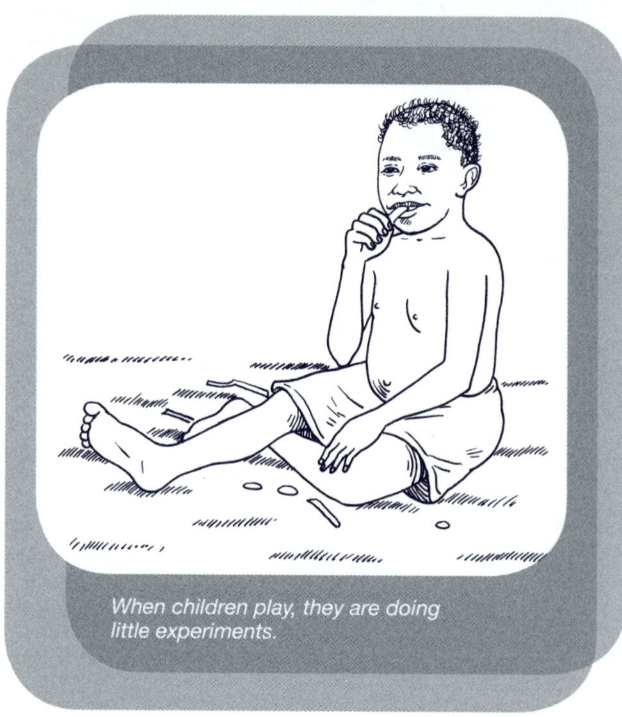

When children play, they are doing little experiments.

As we change from children into **adolescents** and then adults we learn many new things and continue to find out more about the world around us. We continue to do little experiments. For example, we learn that fire is hot and can burn us, so we learn that we should not touch things that are hot. Of course, we don't let babies and small children discover this for themselves because they would get hurt. However, when we are older we might put our hand near something that is hot, or touch it very quickly, in order to find out how hot it is.

As we get older we also try to do things that we have not done before and we learn from the experience. For example, we might learn how to cook food. If you want to cook rice you must decide how much rice to cook, how much water to use, how hot the fire should be and how long to cook the rice. The first time we do it, we might not know what to do and the results might not taste very good. For example, we might add too much water so the rice is too sloppy or we might burn the rice so that it is too dry. However, when we learn from our mistakes we get better each time so that after a while we can do it without thinking and get good results every time.

For you to try

1 Describe some of the new things that you have learned by trying to do them for the first time or by doing little experiments. Include one example where you have learned something by yourself and one where you have learned from somebody else.

Scientific processes

In our everyday lives we are always doing things that help us to understand the world around us. In other words, we are experimenting with the world around us. **Scientists** also carry out experiments to find out about the world around us but they are careful to follow a number of steps called **scientific processes**. When we do the following we are using the processes that we use in science:

- ask questions in order to find an answer
- make **observations**—using all our senses
- carry out experiments or investigations so that we test our ideas
- make measurements using different equipment or instruments
- collect information from our observations and measurements
- record information so that we can organise it, understand it and share it with others
- put things into groups or classify them depending on their characteristics
- solve problems so that we have a better understanding or make our lives easier
- make predictions about what will happen next time or in the future.

For you to try

1 Working in small groups, look through a newspaper and cut out any articles that you think need knowledge of science to help you understand fully. Write one or two sentences explaining why knowledge of science would be helpful in understanding each article.

The scientific method

Over many years scientists have developed a particular way of working and solving problems which is called the **scientific method**. The scientific method usually follows some or all of the following steps:

1 asking a question that guides our observations
2 suggesting a possible answer
3 testing the ideas by doing an experiment
4 recording the results of the experiment
5 checking if the results support the possible answer that was suggested before
6 thinking again and carrying out more experiments if needed
7 making final **conclusions**.

When we use the scientific method we must do the following

- make sure that our experiments are a **fair test**
- be careful in our observations
- collect accurate information
- make good judgments
- have good reasons for the conclusions that we make.

The work of scientists

Science can be divided into a number of different branches, so there are many different kinds of scientists. The table lists the different branches. Scientists are always asking questions about the world around them, and then they try to find answers to their questions. Scientists have found the answers to many questions, but there are many questions yet to be answered. People also keep finding new questions.

Scientists find out about the past

The following example shows the way that the scientific method can be used to help find out about the past:

Branches of science

Branch of science	What is this branch interested in?
Archeology	Finding out about the past and the way that people lived by looking at the things that people have left behind like tools and pottery
Astronomy	The planets, Sun, Moon, stars and the universe
Biology	Living things like plants and animals
Chemistry	Substances like chemicals and medicines and the way that they behave
Ecology	How plants and animals live and interact in the environment
Geology	Rocks and the Earth. Looking for oil and gas.
Health	The reasons why we get sick and how we can get better
Meteorology	The weather, which is caused by what is happening in the atmosphere
Physics	Forces and movement, energy and matter, tools and machines

Science in the village: First agriculture in Papua New Guinea

People in the highlands of Papua New Guinea were some of the first in the world to start making gardens and growing food. In 1966 some people were digging new drainage ditches in the Kuk swamp in the Wahgi valley near Mt Hagen so they could start a tea plantation. When they were digging they found some very old wooden spades and the remains of old drainage ditches.

People who are very interested in finding out about the way that people lived in the past are called **archeologists.** Some archeologists came to the Kuk swamp to look at the evidence and to try to find out more. They used some special tests called carbon dating to work out the age of the wooden spade and found that it was 2300 years old. This was a very exciting discovery.

In 1972, archeologists came back to the Kuk swamp and did some more digging. They were looking for more evidence to help them understand the way that people lived in the past. They found there were many layers of drains at different levels, which showed that people had used the swamp to grow food for a long period of time. They were also able to find out what kind of crops the people had grown. For example, they found that taro was being grown about 10 000 years ago and that banana was being grown from about 7000 years ago. They found the oldest evidence came from the deepest layers and the layers closest to the surface gave evidence that was not so old, so digging into the swamp was like a vertical timeline going back into the past.

They also found layers of volcanic ash at different levels in the soil. Using special tests to work out the age, they found that there had been twenty volcanic eruptions in the area.

Looking at all the evidence from the swamp shows that the Western Highlands is one of first places in the world where people started to grow food crops. This means that agriculture started in Papua New Guinea about 10 000 years ago and this is one of the first examples of it in the world.

For you to try

1 Look at the story 'First agriculture in Papua New Guinea' and answer the following questions:
   - a Why were people digging in the Kuk swamp in 1966?
   - b What evidence did they find?
   - c In 1972, what evidence did the archeologists find?
   - d What conclusions did the archeologists make?

It's not fair!

Most people have a clear idea about what is fair. When you are playing with friends you will probably tell them if they are not being fair, and in return they will tell you if you are not being fair. Playing sport and games is one of the times when we think about being fair. For example, if you want to find the best runners in your school you need to organise some sort of race or competition. The race or competition is a kind of test or experiment. But how do you make sure that the race is fair? You need to think carefully, make some rules or guidelines and tell the runners so that everyone understands that it is fair. For example:

- How long will the race be?
- Where are the start and finish lines?
- Is the race open to all ages or will there be different age groups?
- Will there be separate races for boys and girls?

- How many races will there be? Will there be heats and finals or just one race?
- How do we make sure that runners are not cheating by, for example, jumping the start, cutting corners or short-cutting so that they run a shorter distance?
- What happens to runners who cheat?

You might also think more about the number of races that you have and if you need to repeat the races over a period of time to be fair. For example, what happens if one of the best runners is sick or injured on the day of the race and cannot take part? Or perhaps one of the best runners is unlucky and falls down during the race. Or maybe one runner is doing more training during the term so she becomes much faster. If we repeat the race and compare the results it will help to overcome these differences and find the best runner. The only way to know if the best runner always comes first is to have several races at different times.

Being fair to all runners on a running track

Some sports ovals have a special running or athletics track which is made so that it is fair to all runners. Most running tracks are 400 metres long, with two straights of equal length and two equal curved ends. The track is divided into **lanes** by painting lines on the ground. The 100 metre

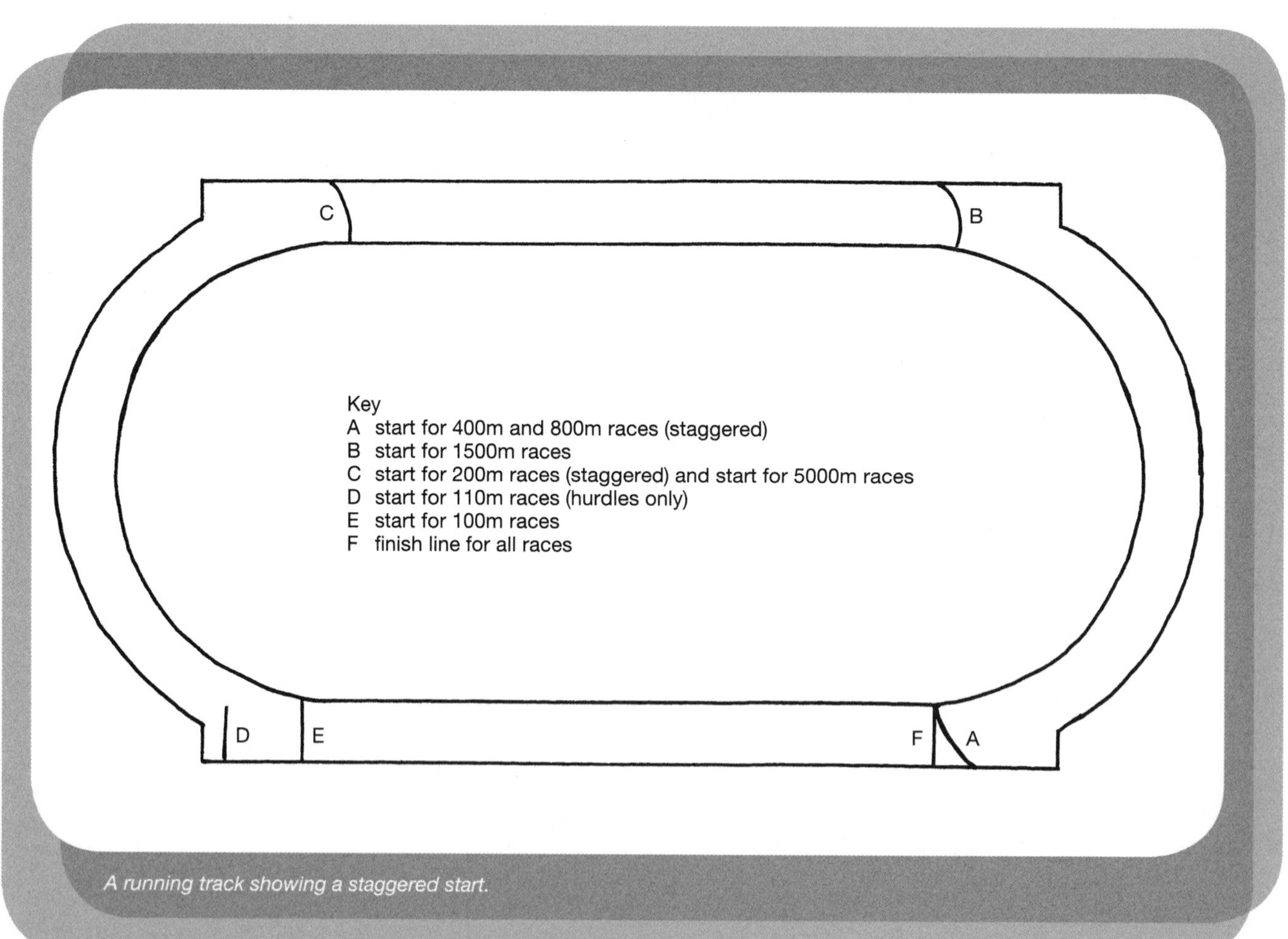

A running track showing a staggered start.

race is held over the straight, and the start line and finish line are the same for everyone. For races of 200 metres, or longer, the curved part of the track is used so the runners start at different points on the curve. This is called a **staggered start**. Each runner must stay in the same lane for the whole race so that they all run the same distance and the finish line is the same for all runners.

Runner stay in the same lane.

For you to try

1. In groups, make a set of rules or guidelines to find the best runners in your school. Use the ideas in the list above and any others that you think are important. Show your rules to other groups. What differences are there in the rules of different groups?
2. Explain why a staggered start is used on a running track for races of 200 metres and longer.
3. If there is a running or athletics track near you, try to visit it with a group of friends. Try to run some races on a running track. Does it make any difference if the runner is on the inside lane, the outside lane, or in the middle?
4. Choose any sport or game and make a list of reasons why it might not be fair to all the players. For example, playing soccer on a field that is not level or holding a fishing competition in which some people use hand lines and some use nets. How can it be made more fair?
5. How does a referee or umpire help to make sure that a game is fair?

Doing a fair experiment

In science we also need to make sure that our experiments are fair and will help us answer our questions or find out what we want to know. There are usually two parts to an experiment, which we do at the same time. One part is called the test, and the other is called the **control**. We compare the results of the test with the results from the control and the difference helps us reach a conclusion. We must always be careful that the conclusion follows from the results.

When the experiment is fair, somebody else should also be able to repeat the experiment and get the same answer, or a similar answer. When different people repeat the same experiment and get the same answer we can feel more confident about our experiments. We can then feel sure that we understand the reasons why something is happening and that nothing is being missed or is hidden.

When we carry out fair experiments the information that we obtain is more likely to be **reliable**. This means that the information is more likely to be true and correct so that we can believe it and trust it.

The following experiments show the importance of using a test and a control in a fair experiment. Some students were trying to find out if stirring makes a difference to the speed that sugar dissolves. Group A and Group B each had the same equipment but did slightly different experiments. The reports of their experiments are shown below:

Group A

Aim To find out if sugar dissolves faster when it is stirred.

Apparatus Two clear glass or plastic containers, watch or clock, warm water, cold water, teaspoon, sugar.

Method
Add about half a cup or 100 mL of warm water to container 1 and the same amount of cold water to container 2.

Add a teaspoon of sugar to each container. Stir both containers in the same way. Measure how long it takes for the sugar to dissolve (or disappear) in both containers.

Results

Container	Time for sugar to dissolve
1 (warm)	20 seconds
2 (cold)	60 seconds

Conclusion Sugar dissolves faster when it is stirred.

Experiment apparatus

Group B

Aim To find out if sugar dissolves faster when it is stirred.

Apparatus Two clear glass or plastic containers, watch or clock, warm water, teaspoon, sugar.

Method
Add about half a cup or 100 mL of warm water to container 1 and the same amount of warm water to container 2.

Add a teaspoon of sugar to each container. Do not stir container 1. Stir container 2 gently to make sure that no water splashes out of the container. Measure how long it takes for the sugar to dissolve (or disappear) in both containers.

Results

Container	Time for sugar to dissolve
1	60 seconds
2	15 seconds

Conclusion Sugar dissolves faster when it is stirred.

Experiment apparatus

Was it a fair experiment?

Did both groups carry out a fair experiment?

Do their conclusions follow from their results?

Group A concluded that stirring helped the sugar to dissolve more quickly. They stirred both containers and looked for differences but they also changed the temperature of the water. They do not know if the sugar dissolved more quickly because of the temperature of the water or because of the stirring. Maybe it was both the temperature and the stirring that helped the sugar dissolve. Their conclusion does not follow from their method and result.

Group B changed only one thing at a time. One container was stirred (the test), and the other was not (the control). They did not change the temperature of the water. It is then fair to say that the difference in the result is due to the stirring.

So the experiment that group B carried out seems like a fair test and the conclusion follows from the result.

For you to try

1 Write some notes for Group A to explain to them how their experiment could be improved. Remember to give reasons for your comments.

Cause and effect

Some of the things that happen have an important **effect** on our lives that we cannot ignore. For example, when there is heavy rain that lasts for many days it affects the lives of people in the **community**. People cannot work in the garden, it is hard to find dry firewood, and it is difficult to move from place to place. When the rain is very heavy, gardens and roads may be washed away and rivers flooded.

We also try to understand the reasons why things happen, or the **cause**. For example, we might try to find out why the rain is always heavy during the same season each year or why the rain is heavy on one side of the mountain, but not on the other side, even though the two places may only be a few kilometres apart.

Scientists can explain the differences in rainfall near mountains in the following way:

- Warm, moist air from the coast blows towards the land and is forced up and over the mountains.
- As the air rises the pressure decreases and the air cools.
- The water vapour in the air condenses to form clouds that produce rain.
- After the air has passed over the mountain it begins to fall down the other side.
- The pressure increases and the air warms up. The cloud evaporates and the air becomes dry, so there is no rain on this side of the mountain. This side of the mountain is in a **rain shadow**.

This kind of rain pattern happens in many parts of Papua New Guinea and it explains why some areas can be very wet, while others nearby are dry.

However, just because two things happen at the same time does not mean that one causes the other. For example, if a tree starts to flower before the wet **season** each year, this does not mean that the flower is making the rain come. However, it might be helpful to the tree to make flowers before the rain showing the tree is in some way 'getting ready' for the rain. The rain will help other plants to grow and these can attract insects which in turn pollinate the flowers of the tree

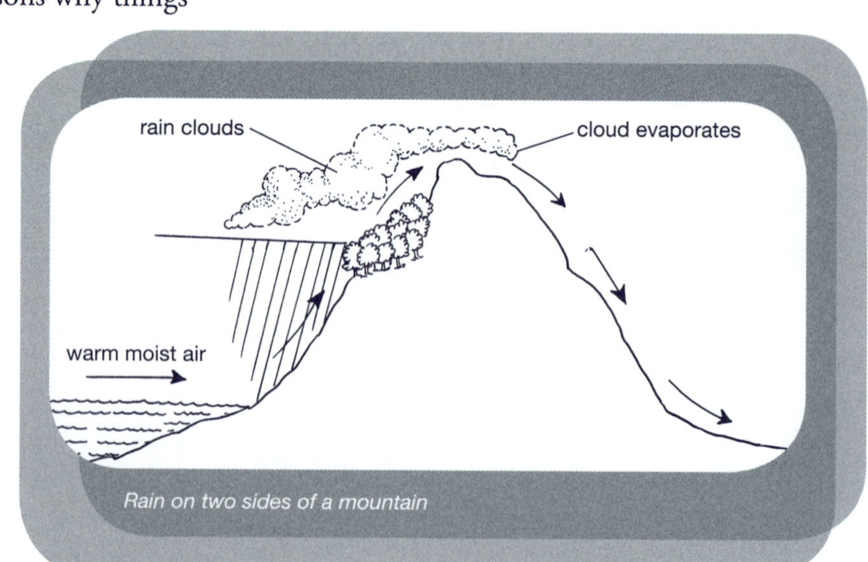

Rain on two sides of a mountain

and make seeds. In this way, when the tree is 'getting ready' for the rain, it helps the tree to be successful.

The scientific method is a good way to understand more about cause and effect. Doing experiments can help us to find out what happens and why this happens.

Steps in doing experiments

Three steps are important when we try to find answers by doing experiments:

1 making observations
2 making an **inference**
3 making a **hypothesis**.

An observation is something that you notice by using any of your senses. We have five senses that send information to the brain. Being observant means using all your senses to notice things around you. It is also important to be careful and accurate in your observations.

Some examples of making observations are:

- smelling onions in the kitchen
- finding that some new material feels smooth and silky
- seeing a boy running away
- hearing a chicken make a lot of noise
- tasting a lemon and finding that it is sour.

An inference is a possible conclusion that follows from information taken from your observations. The inference may be true, or may not be true.

Some inferences that you could make from the observations above are as follows:

- You will have onions with your dinner tonight.
- Your mother bought some material to make a new meri blouse.
- The boy is scared of dogs.
- Someone threw a stone at the chicken.
- Lemons contain an acid.

A hypothesis is a possible explanation that has not been proved. You can test a hypothesis by doing an experiment. Some hypotheses that you could make about the observations above are:

- Onions smell more on a dry day than on a wet day.
- The material feels smooth and silky because the fibres are very small and close together.
- The boy running away was bitten by a dog last year.
- When chickens are frightened they warn each other about the danger.
- Lemons are sour because they contain citric acid.

For you to try

1 Make some different inferences, or possible conclusions, that follow from the list of five observations above.

2 **Investigation: Observing a burning candle**

a Collect a candle and a box of matches.

b Light the candle and observe it carefully.

c Draw a table with two columns, one for observations and one for inferences.

d List six observations of the burning candle and three inferences you can make from your observations.

(continued over)

e Use the diagram below to help you.

3 **Investigation: Thin candles and thick candles**

a In groups, plan an experiment to test the hypothesis that 'thin candles burn faster than thick candles because there is less wax to burn'.

b Your method should include some way of measuring the height of the candles, as well as comparing the mass of the two candles. You will have to make a simple balance and think of some way of comparing the two candles so that you can find out if more wax has been burned in one candle than the other.

c Write down your plan and discuss it with the other groups and with the teacher.

d When you have agreed on your plan, carry it out and write up the experiment in the normal way.

e Remember to say whether the hypothesis is correct or not.

4 **Investigation: Does a lid keep a drink hot for longer?**

a Collect two mugs or cups that are exactly the same, and a lid or saucer.

b Some trade stores sell mugs or cups that have their own lid or you can put a saucer or some other lid on top of a mug of hot tea or coffee.

c Some people believe that a lid helps to keep the drink hot. Does this work?

d In groups, plan an experiment that answers the question.

e Remember that you will need a test and a control.

f Discuss your plan with your teacher.

g Then carry out your planned experiment and write it up.

h Share your conclusions with other groups.

5 **Investigation: Can you make a hot drink cool down more quickly by pouring it into a cold cup?**

a Collect three cups or mugs that are exactly the same; tea, coffee, or Milo; milk or sugar; and cold water in a dish or bucket.

b Label the cups A, B and C.

c Make two cups of tea or coffee, one each in cup A and B. The two hot drinks must be made in exactly the same way.

d Observe both drinks as they cool down under different conditions. You can do this by touching the outside of the cup and taking a sip from each cup.

e Let cup A cool down on its own.

f Let cup B stand for about a minute until the cup is hot.

g Pour the drink from the cup B into the empty cold cup C and let it stand for about a minute. Put the hot cup into the cold water to cool it down.

h Again pour the drink from cup C back into cup B and let it stand.

i Repeat this step again and again until the tea or coffee is cool enough to drink.

j What conclusions can you make about the cooling of the two drinks?

Science in the community

People are interested in the things they find around them and often want to find out more about why things happen and how they work.

Science can help us to understand the world and to improve life in the community.

People who learn science will have a better understanding of what is going on in the world. This can be very useful when you make choices about the way that you live, and when you need to understand information about your environment.

Science can help us to:

- understand how things work, maintain them and fix them when they go wrong, for example, pressure lamps, bicycles and engines.
- use tools to do work, for example, **levers**, the wheel and **axle**, **inclined planes**, **pulleys** and gear wheels
- use technology in our lives, for example, radios, telephones and computers
- grow and prepare good food, and eat a healthy diet
- prevent sickness and know what to do when we get sick, for example, keeping clean and avoiding smoking and chewing betel nut
- make good decisions about the way that we use the environment, for example, fishing, **logging**, mining and getting rid of waste.

The information that we use to make decisions must be reliable. This means that the information must be true and correct so that we can trust it and apply it.

For you to try

1 In groups discuss how science can help people in your community. Make a presentation or share your ideas with other groups.

2 Explain how science can be used to make responsible choices to improve community life.

Projects

1 Making hot food go cold

- a How can you make a saucepan of hot food go cold as quickly as possible?
- b List your ideas and test them by doing experiments.
- c Remember to use a control in each experiment.
- d Write up your project and show your results in a way that is clear for everyone to see.

2 Using science to make life better

- a Brainstorm ideas for a class project in which you make use of science or the scientific method to improve life in the community.
- b Plan and carry out your project with your teacher.
- c The project may last for several weeks or several months.

Summary questions

1 Answer **true** or **false**:

Science is	T or F?
a way of doing things.	
a way of looking at things.	
a way of thinking about things.	

2 Which of the following best describes the way that scientists work and solve problems?

A the scientific method

B method, results and conclusions

C scientific processes

D a way of doing things.

3 Match the steps in the scientific method with the order they are carried out.

Steps in the scientific method	Order
A asking a question that guides our observations	6
B suggesting a possible answer to the question	4
C testing the ideas by doing an experiment	2
D recording the results of the experiment	7
E checking if the results support the possible answer that was suggested before	5
F thinking again and carrying out more experiments if needed	3
G making final conclusions	1

4 The two main parts of a fair experiment are known as:

A method and results

B results and conclusions

C test and control

D experiment and conclusions.

5 Answer **true** or **false**:

When an experiment is fair …	T or F?
somebody else should also be able to repeat the experiment and get the same answer.	
different people can repeat the same experiment and get a different answer, and we can feel more confident about our experiments.	
repeating the experiment can help to understand why something is happening and that nothing is being missed.	

6 Match each word with the meaning in the table:

Word	Meaning	Answer
A control	**1** something that you notice with your senses	
B hypothesis	**2** an experiment or project that you do to answer a question	
C inference	**3** a comparison so that a fair experiment is done	
D investigation	**4** an explanation of what you observed	
E observation	**5** a guess at an answer that you can check by experiment	

7 The passage below is a summary of the main ideas of this chapter. Copy and complete the passage in your book. Using the words in the list, find the words that are missing. You can use each word only once.

choices, conclusion, decide, equipment, experiments, fair, improve, information, method, question, scientific

When we want to find out about something and understand it better, we often carry out ____________ or investigations. Investigations often start with a ____________ or a problem, we choose a ____________ in order to get some results and then we make a ____________. This way of doing things is called the ____________ method. When we are planning an investigation we must make sure that it is ____________ in order to find out why things happen and how they work. We often have to make and use simple ____________ in order to collect information that will help us to carry out investigations. When we have collected ____________ we can use it to make and support a conclusion. After carrying out an investigation we should ____________ whether it was a fair test. Science can be used to ____________ community life by making sure we make responsible ____________ that are based on reliable information.

2

Living things

Chapter summary

In this chapter you will have an opportunity to:

- find out about the structure of living things and how this helps them live in their environment.
- compare the body coverings of animals and find out how these coverings help the animals live in their environment
- collect and use information about the body coverings of animals
- find out about the human digestive system and the way it works
- compare the digestive systems of different animals
- find out about the feeding relationship between plants and animals by making a food web
- find out how human activities affect the environment and share your ideas with other people.

Syllabus references

Strand: Living things

Sub-strands: Nature of living things
Ecology, relationships and interactions

Outcomes:

7.2.1 Identify and compare the basic structure of living things and how they allow them to function in their environment

7.2.2 Interpret and discuss relationships that exist in a community using a food web to show the human activity in that community

Key facts

- The structure of living things helps them to live in the environment.
- The different structures of living things allow them to live in different environments.
- The structure of the different parts of living things is related to the job the part must do.
- All animals have a body covering that is suited to the place where they live.
- The digestive system of humans allows us to break down the food we eat.
- Breaking down food provides us with energy and also produces waste.
- Other animals also have a digestive system. The type of digestive system depends on the kind of food the animal eats.
- The plants and animals living together in an ecosystem are in a feeding relationship called a food web.
- Human beings are also part of a food web and have a relationship with other plants and animals in the environment.
- The activities of humans have a bigger effect on the environment than any other animal because of the way we obtain food and use other resources.

Sorting out plants

There are thousands of different kinds of plants. The structure of plants helps them to live in different environments. We can sort out plants into five main groups according to their structure:

1 Flowering plants

- **Flowering plants** are the largest group of plants.
- All flowering plants have true **roots**, a **stem**, leaves and a flower.
- Most have broad leaves and produce seeds that are covered.
- Some have woody stems, while others have soft stems.
- Most live on land, while some live in water.
- The job of the flowers is to produce seeds, which form inside the fruit.
- When fruits are carried away from the parent plant they will dry and open, letting the seeds go free, which completes the life cycle of the plant.
- Flowering plants include, for example, trees, vegetables, cereal crops, herbs, shrubs and grasses.

2 Conifers

- **Conifers** are plants that have cones.
- Most are evergreen and have narrow leaves shaped like a needle, which means that they lose less water than plants with broad leaves.

Flowering plants have many colours.

A young pine tree

- There are two types of cone—the male cone produces pollen and the female cone produces seeds.
- The small male cones grow each year in groups at the base of new **shoots**.
- Female cones grow for two years, slowly increasing in size.
- Examples of conifers are pine trees, like the hoop pine.

3 Ferns

- **Ferns** are green plants with roots and a short thick underground stem.
- The leaf or frond is the part that is seen above ground.
- New fronds are curled up in tight bundles that unfold and open out.
- Ferns have hard veins or ribs that carry water and food for the plant, and also support the leaves.
- Ferns usually live where it is damp and there is not too much sun.

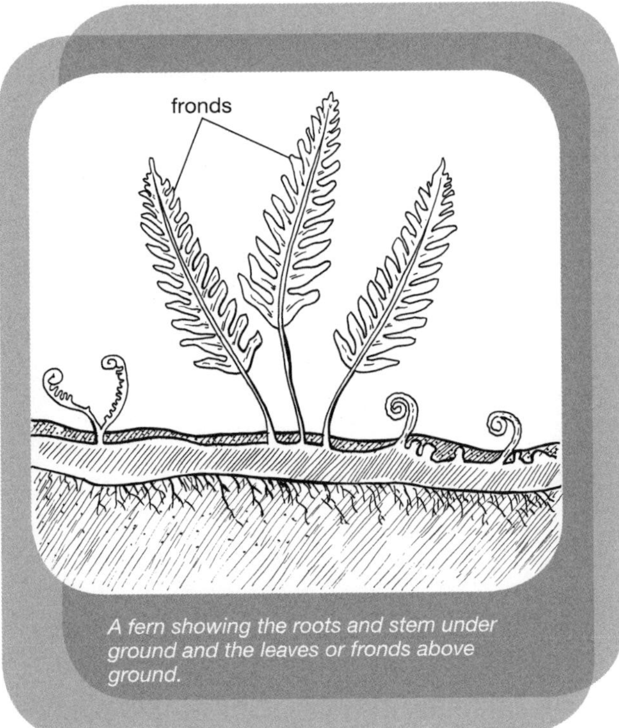

A fern showing the roots and stem under ground and the leaves or fronds above ground.

- Ferns reproduce by means of spores that are brown in colour and are found on the underside of the leaves or fronds.
- Ferns do not have flowers and seeds.
- Examples of ferns are bracken, edible ferns and tree ferns that can grow to 20 metres.

4 Mosses

- **Mosses** are green plants that grow to between 2 and 10 cm tall.
- Some have branches and grow as creepers, others do not have branches and grow like a cushion or a carpet.
- Mosses do not have true roots, stems or leaves, although they have similar structures.
- Mosses feel soft because they contain no fibres or veins.
- **Liverworts** are similar to mosses but have small, flat leaves close to the ground.

Moss plants

5 Algae

- **Algae** grow in water or damp places such as tree trunks, in the soil, and on walls and rocks.
- All algae have **chlorophyll**, but the green colour can be hidden by other colours.
- Algae do not have roots, stems or leaves.
- Examples of algae are seaweed, pond slime and tiny phytoplankton that floats on the surface of the sea and provides a food source for many animals living in the sea.

The diagram below shows the way that we can sort plants into groups according to their structure.

Algae growing in a pond.

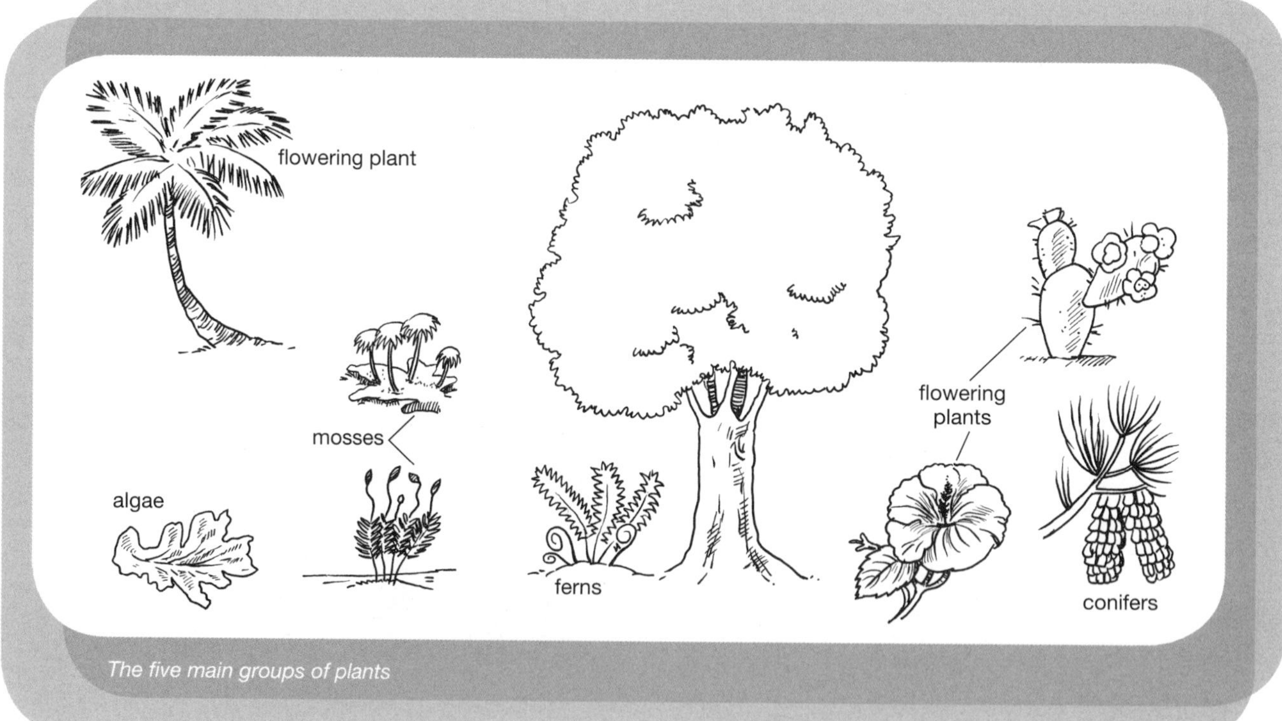

The five main groups of plants

For you to try

1 **Investigation: Finding the height of a tree**

a Collect a metre ruler and a measuring tape. If you do not have a measuring tape, you can use the method below. It will also need to be a sunny day.

b Find a tree in a place where you can easily and safely measure the shadow of the tree.

c Measure the length of the shadow of the tree in metres.

d Place the metre ruler next to the tree so that it casts a shadow. Measure the length of the shadow in metres.

e Divide the length of the shadow of the tree by the length of the shadow of the ruler. The answer will be the height of the tree in metres.

f If you do not have a measuring tape, use a piece of string to find the length of the shadow of the ruler and see how many times this fits into the length of the shadow of the tree. The answer will be the height of the tree in metres.

g Share your results with other groups. Do you agree about the height of the same tree or similar trees?

2 Do the following activity: **The best conditions for seeds to grow well**

a Imagine that you have been given 20 seeds of a special tropical plant that can produce a crop that is worth a lot of money.

b Unfortunately, you do not know the name of the plant so you do not know what conditions will make the plant grow well.

c Design an experiment to find out the best conditions for the seeds to grow well.

d Remember that you will need to use a test and a control for each condition that you want to investigate.

The structure of flowering plants

There are many different types of flowering plants. They provide us with food, clothing, building materials, firewood, rope, dyes and medicine. Flowers are also used to make people look attractive and to decorate buildings on special occasions.

Flowering plants are also important because they make their own food from the air, water and sunlight during the process of **photosynthesis**.

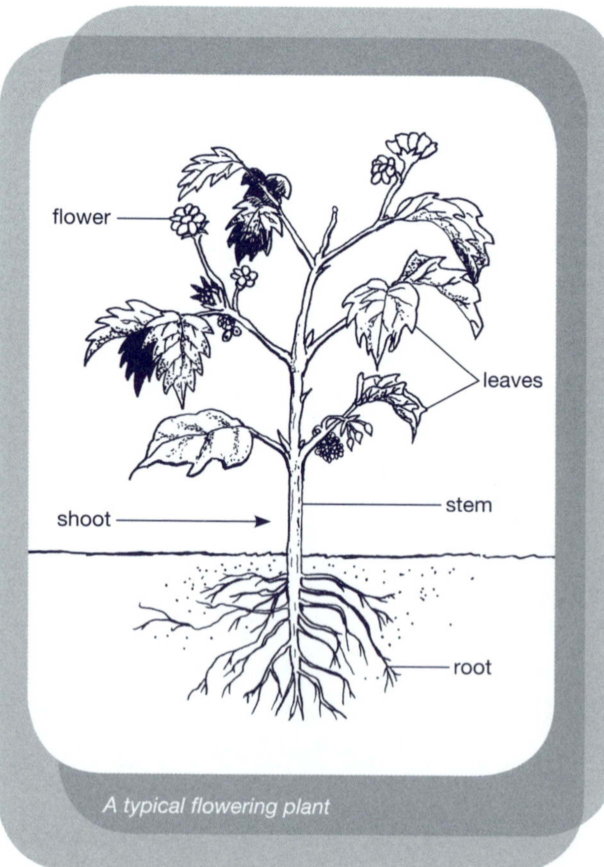

A typical flowering plant

They also provide oxygen which is needed by all living things.

Studying the structure of flowering plants will help us understand the way in which they make their own food and produce oxygen. All flowering plants have the following:

- a shoot, which is the part above the ground with a stem that supports the leaves, buds, flowers and fruits.
- a root, which is the part below the ground

Roots and shoots have characteristics that make them suitable for the kind of job they do and help plants to be successful in their environment. These characteristics are called **adaptations**.

Plants vary in their type of stem, root **system**, shape of leaves, and in many other ways. Scientists call this **variation**. Some examples of variation are given below:

- stems can be
  - horizontal (e.g. couch grass)
  - underground (e.g. bamboo)
  - long and thin (e.g. passion fruit)
- leaves can have
  - parallel veins (e.g. grasses)
  - network veins (e.g. sweet potato)
- roots can have
  - a tap root system (e.g. beans)
  - a fibrous root system (e.g. corn)

A rain tree

A mangrove tree

A coconut tree

A cedar tree

Roots and root adaptations

The main job or function of plant roots is to hold the plant in the ground and support the shoot. Roots also absorb water and mineral salts, which are carried in special tubes to the shoot. However, many plants have roots that are adapted or modified to carry out special functions. Some examples are shown in the table:

Root adaptation	Examples
Food storing roots	yam
Climbing roots	mustard plant
Supporting roots	prop roots of the pandanus buttress roots of rainforest trees
Breathing roots	mangrove
Parasitic roots	strangler fig

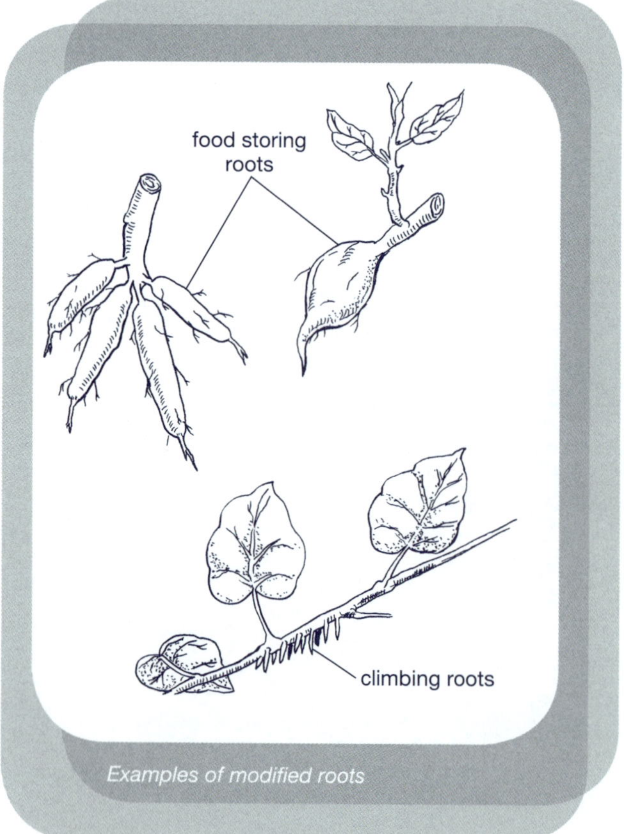

Examples of modified roots

Shoots and shoot adaptations

The stem of a plant must carry water and mineral salts absorbed by the roots to all other parts of the plant. Leaves must receive water and mineral salts so that they can make food. Leaves contain a green **substance** called chlorophyll that uses the **energy** from sunlight to make food during photosynthesis. The stem holds the leaves and spreads them out so that they can receive as much sunlight as possible.

The main function of the leaves is to make food for the whole plant. However, some leaves are adapted or modified for special functions, as shown in the table:

Leaf adaptation	Examples
For water storage	Purslane or Portulaca
For food storage	Onion bulb
For vegetative reproduction	Mother of Thousands, or Bryophyllum
For trapping insects	Venus fly trap
For protection	Outer layers of the onion bulb
Prevention of water loss	Waxy leaves e.g. coconut, galip nut; spines of the cactus
For climbing	Tendrils of the passion fruit
For getting rid of salt	Mangrove

For you to try

1 Investigation: Looking at different plants

a Each group should collect a number or different types of plants. A magnifying glass would also be useful if you have one.

b Number each plant so that the whole class can look at the same set of plants and compare their results.

c Examine each plant carefully and put your results in a table like the one below. Put a tick in the column if the characteristic is present.

d Try to work out which group each plant belongs to.

e Discuss your results with other groups.

Plant types							
Plant no.	Stem	Leaves	Roots	Cones	Flower	Colour	Type
1							
2							
3							
4							
5							

2 Look at the chart 'The five main groups of plants', and answer the following questions:

a What type of plant has seeds in cones, roots, a woody stem, and no flowers?

b What type of plant has no true roots, stems or leaves?

c What type of plant has no stem, simple roots and no leaves?

d What type of plant has seeds, roots, stems and flowers?

e Which plant groups would you classify as non-flowering?

f Which two plant groups produce seeds? What are the differences between these two groups?

g Ferns and mosses both produce spores, but mosses grow very close to the ground while ferns grow much higher above the ground. What part of the plant allows ferns to grow so much taller than mosses?

h How could you tell the difference between pond slime that you find on a rock, and a moss?

i Why do conifers have two types of cones?

Project: Growing native trees

a Collect seeds from native trees that grow in your area or another area, and pots or containers with holes for drainage and some soil.

b Plant the seeds and label the pot or container with the name of the tree and the date the seed was planted.

c Make a nursery outside where the containers can get enough sunlight. If the sun is too strong you may have to make some shade for the seedlings.

d Take care of the seedlings and make sure that they get enough water and are not damaged by heavy rain or wind.

e Observe the different seedlings and make some comparisons. Which trees grow the fastest? Which trees produce the most leaves and the most shade? How do the stem and leaves of a young tree change as it grows?

f When the trees are big enough plant them out in the school or in the community. Remember to choose a suitable place where the tree can grow to its full size.

g When you have a special day at your school with visitors from outside you may be able to sell some of the young trees or give them as presents to people.

Science in the village: Using plants that we don't eat

Plants are our most important source of food, but we also use plants in many different ways. It is usually the structure or the properties of the plant that makes it useful. For example:

Fibres are very important to make string or rope for tying things together, for weaving and making clothes. Most fibres come from the bark of trees. The bark is stripped in sheets that are then beaten to separate the fibres. After cleaning, the fibres are separated, straightened and carefully rolled and twisted together. This work needs a lot of skill and is usually done by women. The strongest fibre comes from the bark of the Gnetum tree. The best bilums that are used to carry children and vegetables from the garden are made of Gnetum. The bark of the hibiscus tree is also used by coastal people to make strong string for tying outrigger and sailing canoes.

Tapa cloth is made from the bark of a fig tree. Large sheets of bark are taken from the tree and beaten carefully to separate the fibres and keep the non-fibrous material between the fibres. Various patterns are made using dyes made from plants or ones that are bought from trade stores.

Traditional dress can be made from many different plants, depending on the area.

Fibres from bark are made into shawls and aprons, like those in Enga and other highland provinces.

Beaten bark is made into capes e.g. the Kukukuku people of Eastern Highlands.

Pandanus leaves are sewn together to make a rain cape in Enga.

Gourds are used by men to cover the penis in Telefomin and other places.

Grasses and sedges are used to make skirts and are sometimes specially grown in Enga. Leaves from the banana are used to make grass skirts in the Trobriand Islands.

Bark belts are worn by men in Enga, Chimbu and other parts of the highlands.

Decoration Brightly coloured leaves and flowers are often worn in the hair. For example, hibiscus is often used in this way on the coast. The small, hard, grey grass seeds that are known as Job's tears are worn as headbands, chest ornaments and as strings of beads in the highlands.

Dyes Plant dyes are used for giving different colours to tapa cloth and bilums.

Cooking and eating Bamboo is used to carry water and for cooking. Food bowls and plates can be carved from special trees. The shell of the coconut is use to make drinking cups and containers for carrying water.

Building materials Many different plants are used in different parts of the country to build houses. For example, kwila and mangrove can be used for posts, split palm can be used on the floor, woven bamboo can be used for walls, and the roof can be made from sago or nipa palm, woven coconut or kunai grass. Special logs and the kunda cane are also used to build bridges.

Drums The kundu drum is made from the kundu tree and the garamut is made from the garamut tree.

Canoes are made from different trees and the ones used on rivers are often just made from one big log. Coastal canoes usually have an outrigger to make it more stable.

Gums and resins from trees like the rosewood and fig tree are used as glue and to tune kundu drums.

Sorting out animals

We can sort animals into different groups according to their structure. Animals without backbones or **skeletons** are called **invertebrates**, although some invertebrates such as crabs, crayfish and beetles have external skeletons. Invertebrates are the biggest group of animals. Animals with backbones or internal skeletons are called **vertebrates**. When we look more carefully at vertebrates we find that they have different body coverings and this helps us to sort them into five smaller groups: birds, **mammals**, fish, **reptiles** and **amphibians**.

Birds

- A bird is any animal that has feathers. Feathers allow birds to fly and keep warm and dry. Birds have glands that produce a special oil that is spread over the feathers to make them waterproof.
- All birds have wings and most can fly but some cannot, for example, the cassowary. **Strong** light bones also help birds to fly.
- Birds also have feet with claws, and scales on their legs.
- Birds are warm-blooded and lay eggs with hard shells. The eggs must be kept warm until they hatch. Most birds take care of their young.
- Many birds eat insects, seeds and fruits. Some birds eat flesh or meat and some eat fish.
- Birds have lungs to breathe.
- Birds can have many different colours. Bright colours have probably developed as a way to identify each other and attract mates. Some birds have colours and patterns that make them difficult to see. This is called **camouflage** and it helps protect them against **predators**.
- Birds have many different types of songs and these are used to communicate with each other. For example, birds often mark their **territory** by singing and can also warn each other of danger.
- Papua New Guinea has many birds that have been declared national animals and are therefore protected. For example, the thirty-two birds of paradise, goura pigeons, egrets and ospreys are protected species.
- The cassowary is the most dangerous bird in the world. Their strong legs and big claws

The cassowary has a bony plate on top of its head.

mean that a kick from a cassowary can injure or even kill another animal or a person. The cassowary also has a bony plate on the top of its head that helps it push through the bush.

For you to try

1 How is the cassowary suited or adapted to the environment in which it lives?

2 Why is it helpful for birds to be able to mark their territory by singing and telling other birds that they are there?

Mammals

- A mammal is any animal that has fur or hair on the body. Mammals also have two pairs of limbs.
- Mammals are warm blooded and most have sweat glands to help them cool down when they are hot.

The dugong is an unusual Papua New Guinean mammal.

- All mammals have lungs to breathe, including whales, dolphins, seals and dugongs; they have to be able to hold their breath for a long time when they are under water.
- The dugong is a sea mammal that eats sea grasses found in shallow water. In 1976, it was made a national animal of Papua New Guinea because people were worried that numbers were decreasing. There is also a law that says that dugongs can only be hunted by traditional methods.
- All mammals are born alive except for the platypus and echidna (or spiny anteater). The echidna is one of the national animals of Papua New Guinea.
- Young mammals are fed on mother's milk and parents care for their young for a period of time.
- Mammals can be divided into three groups: **monotremes**, **marsupials** and **placentals**.

Groups of mammals		
Mammal type	Main features	Examples
monotreme	egg laying	echidna (spiny anteater), platypus
marsupial	young develop in pouch	kangaroo, wallaby, possum, bandicoot
placental	young develop in mother's womb before being born alive	rat, cat, dog, pig, human, whale

Human beings

Human beings are mammals. Humans have a backbone, hair on the body and produce milk for the young. Babies are born alive and are looked after by their parents for a long time—longer than any other animal.

Humans are the most highly developed of all animals and are able to do many things that other animals cannot. This is because humans have developed a very complex brain and nervous system. Because of this humans are able to think, talk, read and write.

The **development** of this complex brain means humans can make and use tools. With tools people have been able to change the environment. Land can be cleared and food grown. Many **machines** have been developed that help us survive. Humans have changed the environment more than any other animal.

A chimpanzee and a human – both are mammals.

For you to try

1 What are three characteristics that all mammals have in common?
2 How are marsupials like the wallaby different from other mammals?
3 Dolphins and whales are mammals. In what ways are they like fish? In what ways are they like other mammals?
4 Some mammals are herbivores, eating only plants. Name three mammals that are herbivores.
5 Choose a mammal and explain how it has adapted to live in its environment.

Fish

- Fish have a **streamlined** body that allows them to move easily through the water.
- Fish have fins that are used for swimming in water.
- Fish are cold-blooded so their body temperature changes with the surroundings.
- Most fish get their oxygen from the water using their **gills**. Oxygen from the water is absorbed into the bloodstream in the gills as water passes over them.
- Most fish reproduce by laying eggs but some sharks and rays give birth to live young.
- The colours and patterns on the bodies of some fish help them to blend with their surroundings and hide from predators. This is called camouflage.
- Fish have good eyesight, a good sense of smell and can feel the movement of objects in the water.
- There are two groups of fish: **bony fish** and **cartilaginous fish**.

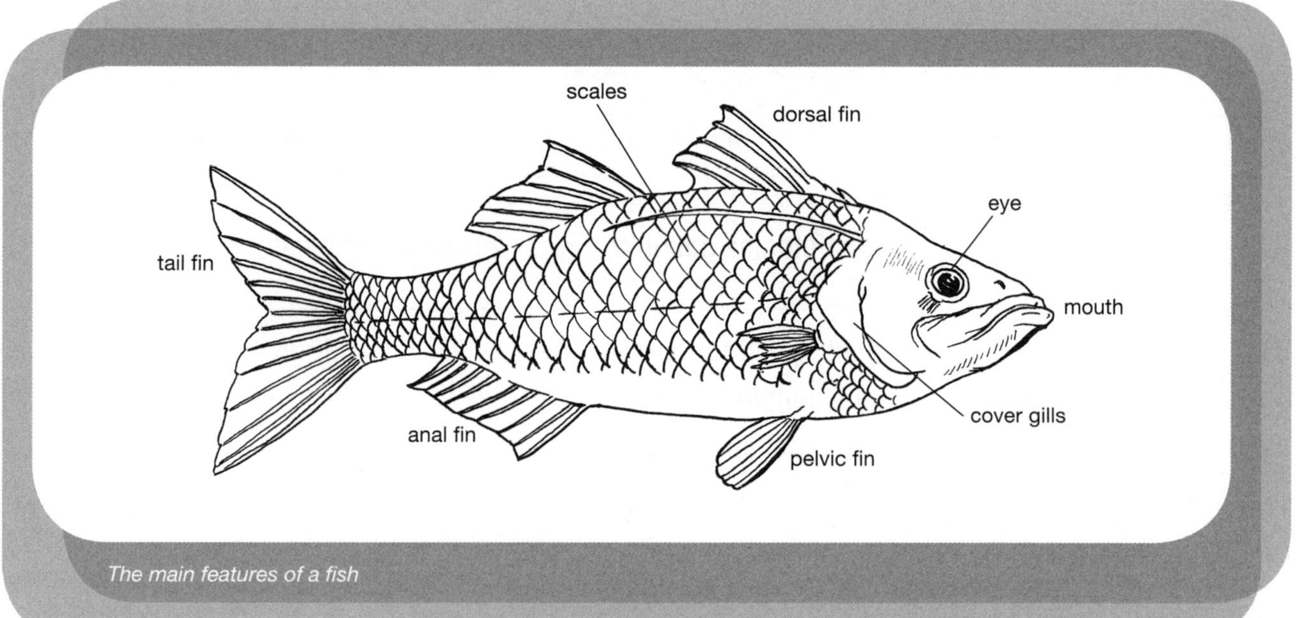

The main features of a fish

- Most fish are bony fish. They have bony skeletons and flat scales all over their bodies. They have a swim bladder which can be filled with air to allow the fish to rise or sink. Examples of bony fish include tuna, mackerel, coral trout, red emperor and tilapia.
- Cartilaginous fish have a skeleton made of cartilage or gristle. Their skin is covered with rough scales. They must keep swimming or they will sink to the bottom. Examples of cartilaginous fish are sharks, skates and rays.
- Fish can live in fresh and salt water and are an important source of food for many people.

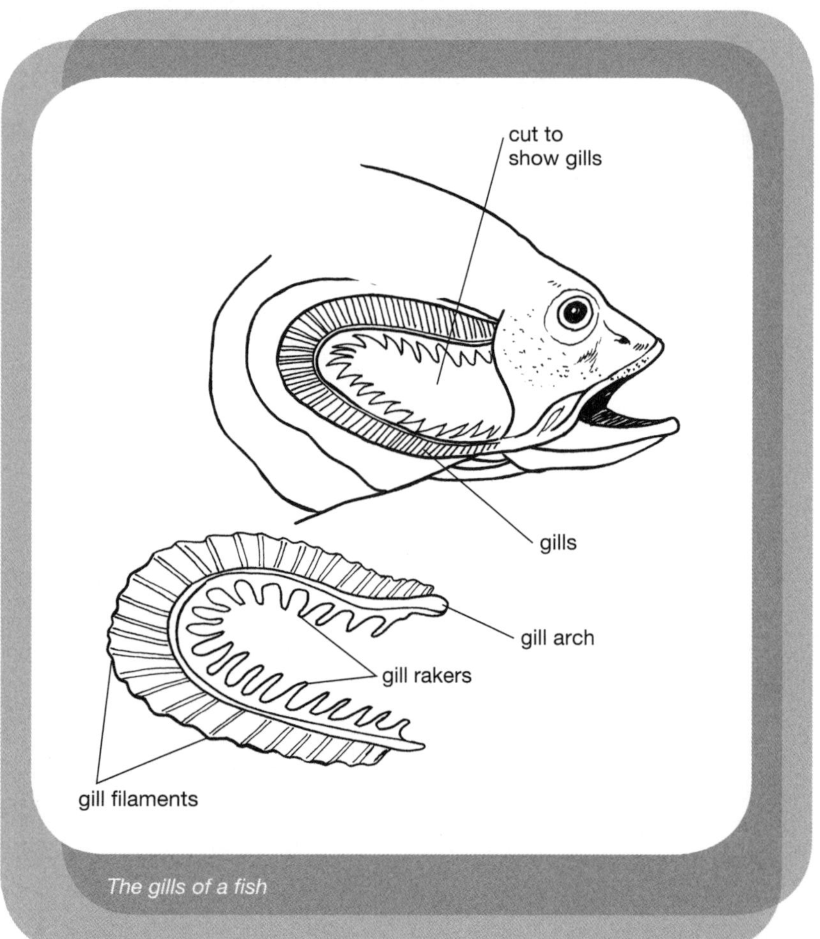

The gills of a fish

For you to try

1 **Investigation: Observing a fish**

- **a** Collect a small fish and put it in jar of water so that you can easily observe it. Remember to put the small fish back where you found it when you have finished. Alternatively, you can observe a bigger fish that has been caught in the sea, a river or lake.
- **b** Use the diagram on page 33 to find the following: dorsal fin, pectoral fin, pelvic fin, anal fin, and caudal fin.
- **c** What covers the body of the fish?
- **d** Where are the gills? What colour are the gills?
- **e** Describe the colour and pattern of the dorsal (back) and ventral (belly) surfaces of the fish.
- **f** Make a drawing of the fish and label as many parts as you can.

2 List the ways in which fish are adapted to living in water.

Reptiles

- Reptiles are cold-blooded and live mainly on land, although crocodiles, turtles and sea snakes live in water. Reptiles move into the sun to get warm and move to the shade to cool down.
- Most reptiles lay eggs but some, such as the tiger snake, give birth to live young. The eggs are usually buried and left so the parents do not take care of them.
- Reptiles have dry, scaly skin and lungs for breathing.
- Reptiles have tongues that can flick in and out very quickly. The tongue is a sense **organ** that is used to find out about the environment.
- This group has many different animals with different characteristics. They have different body structures, different methods of movement and may eat different types of food. Some reptiles are **herbivores**, others are **carnivores**.

Crocodiles

- Crocodiles are the largest living reptiles. They feed on fish, frogs and birds, and will also eat humans.
- There are two types of crocodile: saltwater and freshwater.

Lizards

- Lizards and snakes are the most common reptiles living today. Lizards have legs but snakes do not.
- From time to time lizards lose their outer skin, or **moult**. A new skin grows under the old one before moulting.
- The body or trunk of a lizard has four limbs, each ending in five digits. Each digit has a friction pad and a claw. The friction pads allow some lizards like geckoes to walk upside down on the roof or ceiling.
- Many lizards are able to make their tail drop off in order to distract an enemy. They are then able to grow a new tail.

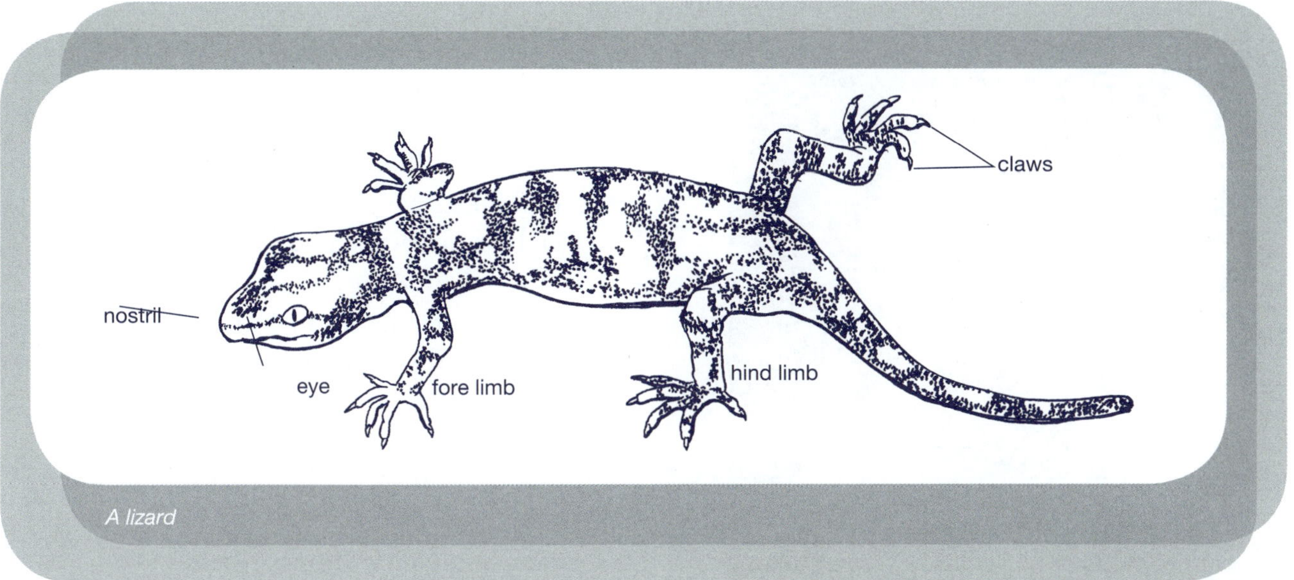

A lizard

For you to try

1 Investigation: Looking at a lizard

- **a** Collect a large glass jar, a piece of paper and an elastic band. Put holes in the piece of paper to make a lid that will allow air to go inside the jar. Collect a gecko or other small lizard and put it in the glass jar.
- **b** Carefully observe the skin, head and feet of the lizard.
- **c** Notice how the lizard moves.
- **d** Make a drawing of the lizard and label the different parts.
- **e** Remember to let the gecko or other small lizard go free as soon as you have finished looking at it.

Snakes

- Snakes do not have legs but they do moult or shed their skin.
- Most reptiles are harmless, but many snakes produce poison that can kill easily. Other snakes, such as the pythons, crush and then swallow their **prey**.
- There are six dangerous snakes in Papua New Guinea: the Papuan black snake, the Papuan taipan, the Papuan whip snake, the death adder, the small-eyed snake and the brown snake.
- The Papuan black, Papuan taipan and Papuan whip snake are found in the Papuan region only.
- The brown snake is the most dangerous snake in Australia, where it is very common, and a few have been found in Milne Bay Province.
- The death adder and the small eyed snake are found all the over the country and are much feared.

A snake

- Snakes are usually shy and will avoid people. For example, they can hear people walking in the bush and will stay away. People who try to catch snakes or play with them are more likely to be bitten.

For you to try

1 Name four types of reptiles. Where does each one normally live and how does it move?

2 Why is it possible for a gecko to walk up walls and to walk upside down on the roof or ceiling?

3 What kinds of reptiles are eaten in your area, or in an area that you know well?

4 Make a simple set of rules for staying safe where there are snakes. In what season are snakes most commonly seen in your area?

Amphibians

- The word **amphibian** means to live on land and in the water. To do this amphibians have special structures for obtaining oxygen.
- Amphibians have skin that is moist, can be rough or smooth, and does not have scales, feathers, hair or fur.
- They can breathe through their skin when in water, and through their lungs and moist skin when on land.
- Amphibians are the smallest group of vertebrates and are cold-blooded. Their body temperature changes with the surroundings.
- Examples of amphibians are frogs, toads, newts and salamanders, although newts and salamanders look more like reptiles.
- All amphibians live in or near water. Most amphibians need to return to the water to lay their eggs, which are protected by jelly.
- The eggs grow into tadpoles that breathe using gills and then develop into young frogs that breathe using lungs. After the lungs have developed the young frog can move out of the water.

A salamander

- In Papua New Guinea, because of the high rainfall and high humidity about half of the frogs lay eggs in damp moss or leaf litter and do not have to return to the water. This means that not all frogs go through the tadpole stage.
- Young amphibians, like tadpoles, feed on water plants, but most adults feed on insects and worms. The adults have sticky tongues that move in and out very quickly and can be used to catch food.
- The cane toad is an amphibian that has been introduced to Papua New Guinea and is now a pest that is found in large numbers all over the country. It produces a poison, so other animals will not eat it.

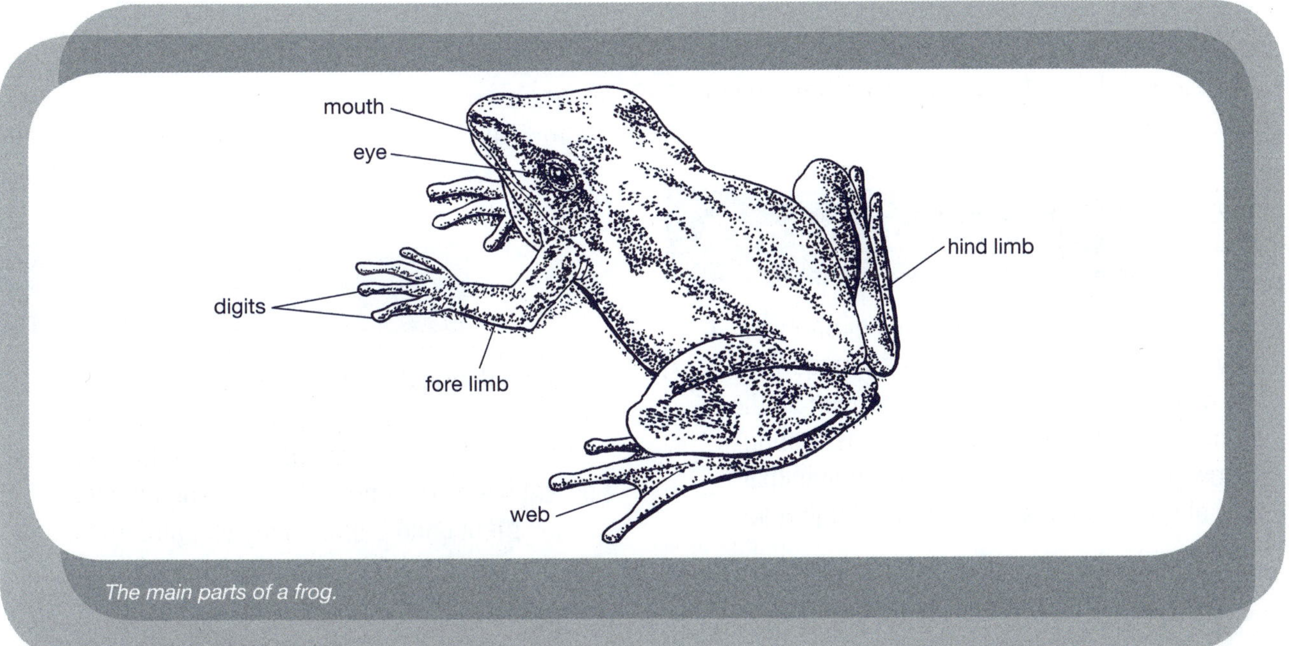

The main parts of a frog.

For you to try

1 **Investigation: Observing a frog**

a Collect a large glass jar, a piece of paper and an elastic band. Put holes in the piece of paper to make a lid that will allow air to go inside the jar. Collect a frog and put it in the glass jar.

b Observe the frog and use the diagram above to look for the following:

- ☐ How many limbs does the frog have?
- ☐ Does the frog have toes?
- ☐ Does the frog have **webbed feet** (skin between the toes)
- ☐ How is the fore limb different from the hind limb?
- ☐ Which limbs are used for jumping and swimming?

c Let the frog out and try to observe how it moves.

d Remember to put the frog back where you caught it when you have finished.

2 How are amphibians like the frog adapted to the way they live in the environment?

Sorting out vertebrates

The following key uses the main characteristics of vertebrates to find which of the five main groups any vertebrate belongs to.

Key for the classification of animals with backbones			
1	a b	feathers on body? → no feathers →	birds go to 2 →
2	a b	hair or fur on body? → no hair or fur on body →	mammals go to 3 →
3	a b	fins on body? → no fins →	fish go to 4 →
4	a b	dry skin → moist skin →	reptiles amphibians

For example, we can use the key to find the group to which a turtle belongs.

First, we start at number 1 in the key and ask ourselves if a turtle has feathers. No, it has not, so we move to number 2 in the key. Next we ask if a turtle has hair or fur. No, it has not, so we move to number 3 in the key. Does the turtle have fins? No, it does not, although it does have legs. So we move to number 4 in the key. Does a turtle have dry skin? Yes, it does, so a turtle is a reptile.

A turtle

For you to try

1 Copy and complete the following table to compare the body coverings of different animals and the way they are suited to the environment. Remember to write the name of your example in the first column.

Animal group and example	Body covering	How is the body covering suited to the environment?
Birds e.g.		
Mammals e.g.		
Fish e.g.		
Reptile e.g.		
Amphibian e.g.		
Invertebrate e.g. crab, crayfish		

2 A student sorted six living things into two groups.

Group A	Group B
frog	mosquito
dog	bird of paradise
dugong	birdwing butterfly

What characteristics have been used to sort the animals?

3 What characteristics do snakes and worms have in common? Why are they placed in different groups?

4 Work out a method for sorting the following living things into three separate groups:

barramundi, cat, crow, dog, eagle, flying fox, elephant, goat, horse, pig, possum, salmon, seal, trout, shark, tuna, wallaby, whale.

Adaptations for feeding

Animals have many different adaptations for feeding. Scientists believe that these adaptations have developed slowly over millions of years to suit different feeding methods.

Insects

The mouth parts of insects are usually arranged for one of the following:

- chewing, as in grasshoppers
- sucking, as in bees
- piercing and sucking, as in mosquitoes.

The grasshopper has powerful jaws that are used to cut the plants on which it feeds. The grasshopper also has mouth parts that hold the food steady and push the food into the jaws as the grasshopper chews.

The bee has the same basic mouthparts as the grasshopper but the jaws are very small. Bees do not chew plants but suck nectar with their mouth tubes. The bee has a mouth tube instead of a lower lip (as in the grasshopper).

Mosquitoes also suck juices through a mouth tube. However, mosquitoes usually feed on the

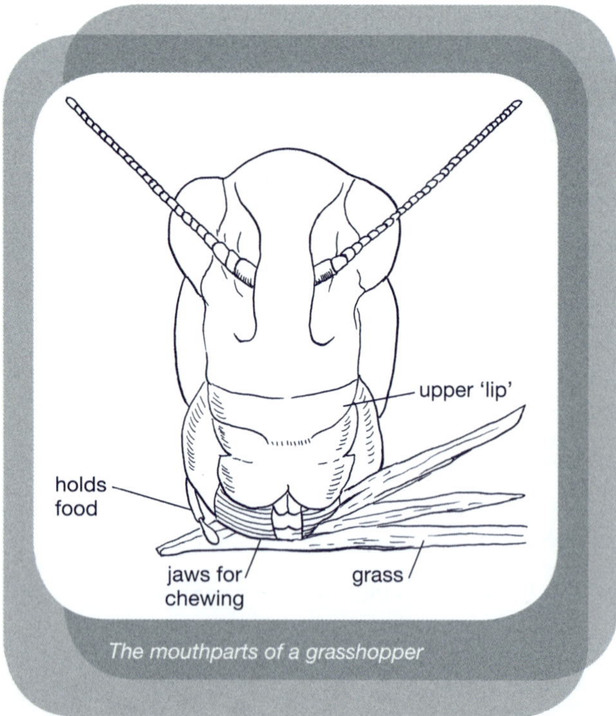

The mouthparts of a grasshopper

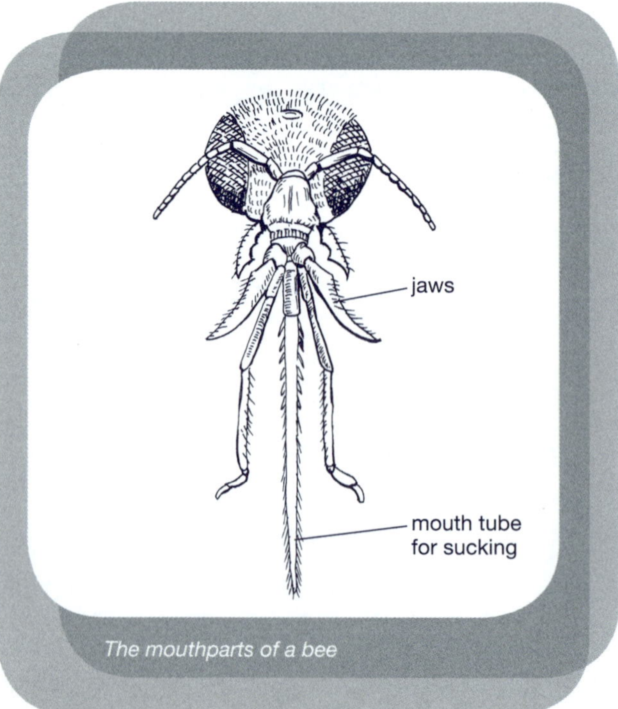

The mouthparts of a bee

juices of plants and blood of animals. To do this, they pierce a hole with two mouth parts that have a serrated edge, like a saw.

Insects can usually be divided into one of four types of feeders.

Plant feeders

About half of all insects feed on plants. This is why they are such a pest because they spoil our crops by eating them or stopping them from growing properly. Examples of plant feeders include grasshoppers, caterpillars and aphids.

Predators

Many insect predators kill and eat other insects. One of the best known is the praying mantis. The adaptations of the praying mantis for feeding are its head which can move very easily, strong jaws and strong front legs with spines that can hold the prey firmly.

Parasites

Parasites get their food and shelter from another living thing called the host. Because the parasite lives on the host, the host suffers and might die. Parasites can live on the outside of or inside the host. For example, the cattle tick lives on the outside of its host. It has mouthparts that bury under the skin and suck out the blood. For this reason it is very difficult to remove. Other insect parasites with similar biting and holding mouthparts are the head louse and the flea.

Scavengers

Animals that help to break down the bodies of dead **organisms** are called **scavengers**. For example, ants have strong mouthparts to tear away pieces of a dead body to take back to their nest. Flies lay eggs in the bodies of dead animals. The eggs hatch and the maggots eat the rotting body.

Birds

Birds have different kinds of beaks depending on what they eat. These different adaptations are shown in the table below:

Type of beak	Adaptations	Examples
Seed-eating beak	Short, thick and strong. Used for crushing and cracking dry seeds.	Lory, parrot, cockatoo, mannikin
Insect-eating beak	Long, narrow and finely pointed, especially if the insects are small or live in crevices.	Sickle bill, birds of paradise, honeyeater
Flesh-eating beak	Quite short and thick with a sharp, hooked tip on the upper bill for pulling meat off bones.	Crested hawk, owl, eagle, kestrel
Water-bird beak	Long, narrow beak suitable for picking animals out of the water.	Heron, egret, kingfisher
	Broad, flat beak to scoop up water plants or take in and sieve mouthfuls of mud. The lower bill may be serrated so that mud passes out but small animals are held.	Duck
Beak for catching insects in flight	Large beak that can open very wide.	Swallow, swiftlet, drongo, fly-catcher
Digging beak	Spade-like beak for digging in the ground.	Wagtail, magpie, starling
Nectar-eating beak	A narrow, tapering beak with a long narrow tongue for drinking nectar from flowers.	Sunbird, honey-eater, humming bird

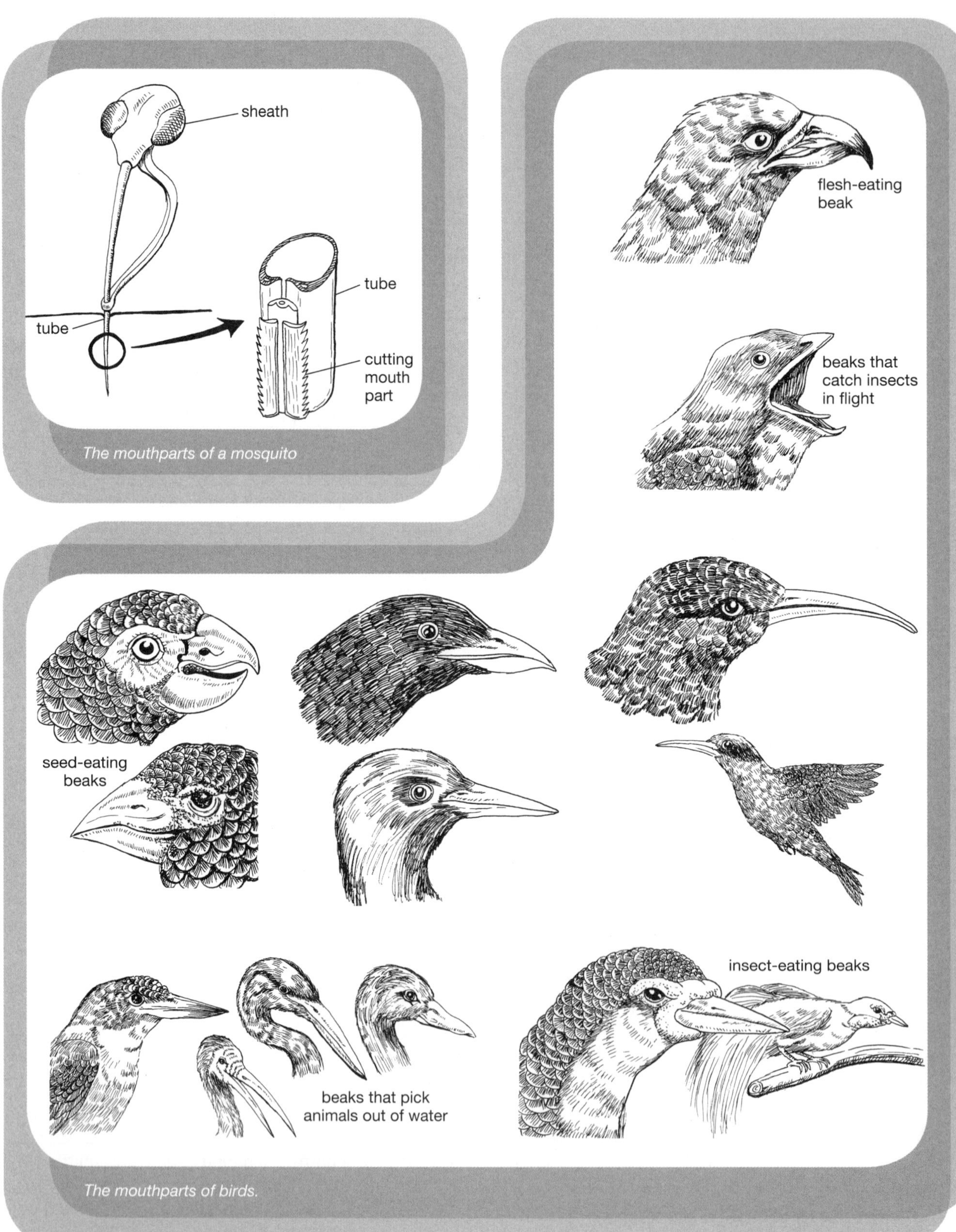

The mouthparts of a mosquito

The mouthparts of birds.

Mammals

Mammals have teeth to help break down the food into smaller pieces, which helps in the process of **digestion**. Most mammals have four kinds of teeth that do different jobs:

- **Incisors** These are sharp-edged, chisel-like teeth at the front of the mouth used for biting off pieces of food.
- **Canines** These are pointed teeth next to the incisors and are used for gripping.
- **Premolars** These are large teeth at the back of the mouth used for crushing.
- **Molars** These are similar to the premolars.

Mammals have three different patterns of teeth, depending on the type of food they eat. This means that we can look at the skull of a dead animal and work out what kind of food it ate.

Carnivores eat meat and have incisors for gripping, and large canines for holding and tearing their food. They have premolars and molars for slicing off flesh and cracking bones. Examples of carnivores are dogs and cats.

Herbivores eat plants and do not have canines because they do not need them. They have sharp incisors for cutting plants, and molars and premolars with sharp ridges on the surfaces. These teeth are needed for crushing plant **cells** and chewing because the plant cell wall is made of a tough substance called **cellulose**. Examples of herbivores are sheep, cows and cus cus.

Omnivores eat both meat and plants. The incisors and canines are similar and are used for biting off pieces of food. The molars and pre-molars are used for grinding food. Examples of omnivores are humans and pigs.

Mammals are different from other animals because they have two sets of teeth. The first set is called the **milk teeth**. In humans, they begin to fall out about the age of seven, after which the permanent teeth grow.

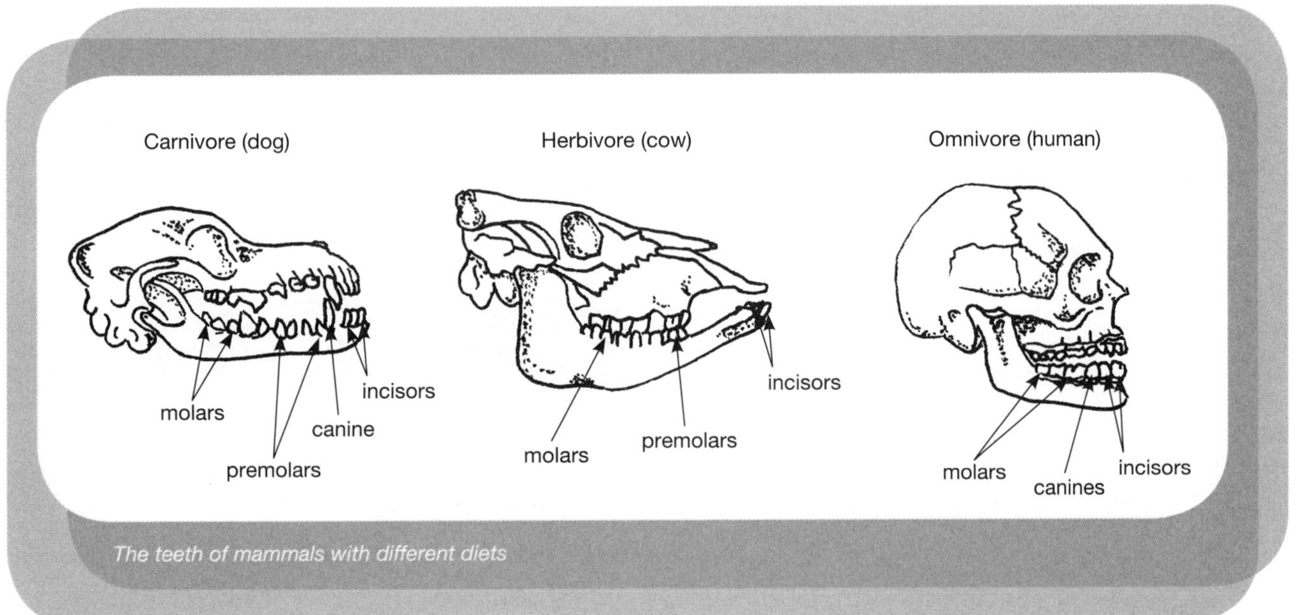

The teeth of mammals with different diets

Care of teeth

A good diet helps human teeth to grow strong. The milk teeth develop before a baby is born and because of this mothers must have plenty of foods containing protein and calcium. Foods such as milk, cheese and beans contain useful amounts of calcium. For the same reason, children should also eat protein foods and foods containing calcium.

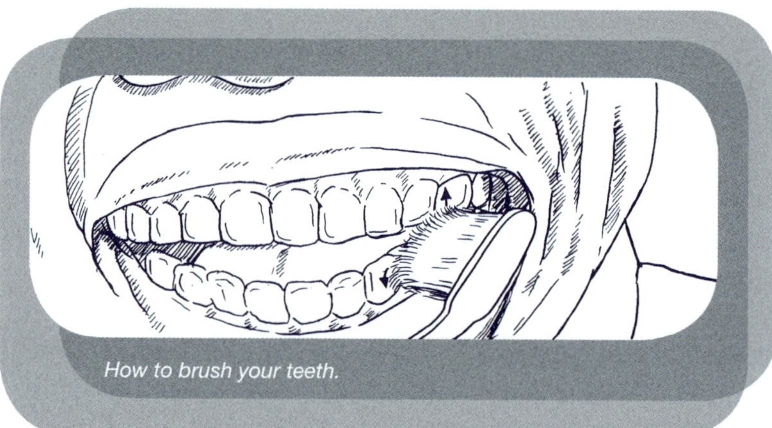

How to brush your teeth.

Cleaning teeth

Teeth cleaning is very important and should be started as soon as a baby starts eating solid food. Cleaning babies' teeth should be done with a soft brush. As a child gets older, stronger brushes and toothpaste should be used. Toothpastes that contain fluoride are best as they help to prevent decay.

How to care for your teeth

1 Avoid eating sweet foods between meals.

2 Avoid drinking sweet fizzy drinks like soft drinks or 'lolly water' because it leads to tooth decay.

3 Brush your teeth at least once per day. The best time is before you go to bed.

4 Brush your teeth firmly, but not roughly, for three to four minutes each time you brush them. Make sure that all parts of the teeth are brushed. Move the brush so that the bristles go into the space between the teeth and the gums.

5 Avoid chewing betel nut and lime which damages the teeth and the gums and may cause the teeth to fall out. Betel nut chewing can also cause mouth cancer.

6 Do not open bottles using your teeth because it can damage them.

7 Visit the dentist regularly, if possible. This will allow any tooth decay and gum disease to be found at an early stage.

For you to try

1 Make a list of the main things you need to remember to keep you teeth and gums healthy.

2 Describe the ways in which the food of mammals is related to the types of teeth they have.

The digestive system

Animals have organs and **tissues** that work together as a system to carry out a particular job or function. For example, all vertebrates have a **digestive system**, which is a tube that starts at the mouth and ends at the anus. The food that animals eat provides energy that is needed for such things as moving, breathing, growing and thinking. Every cell of an animal's body needs energy.

Digestion is the breakdown of large particles of food into small, simple particles. The small particles can then be absorbed by the blood and carried to all cells of the body. Digestion occurs in two stages:

1 mechanical or physical digestion using teeth and muscles
2 chemical digestion using special chemicals called **enzymes**.

The digestive system of vertebrates is divided into the following parts, as shown with the example of the human system:

1 The mouth, which consists of the lips, teeth, tongue and cheeks, breaks up the food mechanically. An enzyme called **amylase** also begins the chemical breakdown of starch.
2 The **gullet** contains muscles that move food in a tube from the mouth to the **stomach**.
3 The stomach is where mechanical digestion occurs with muscles churning

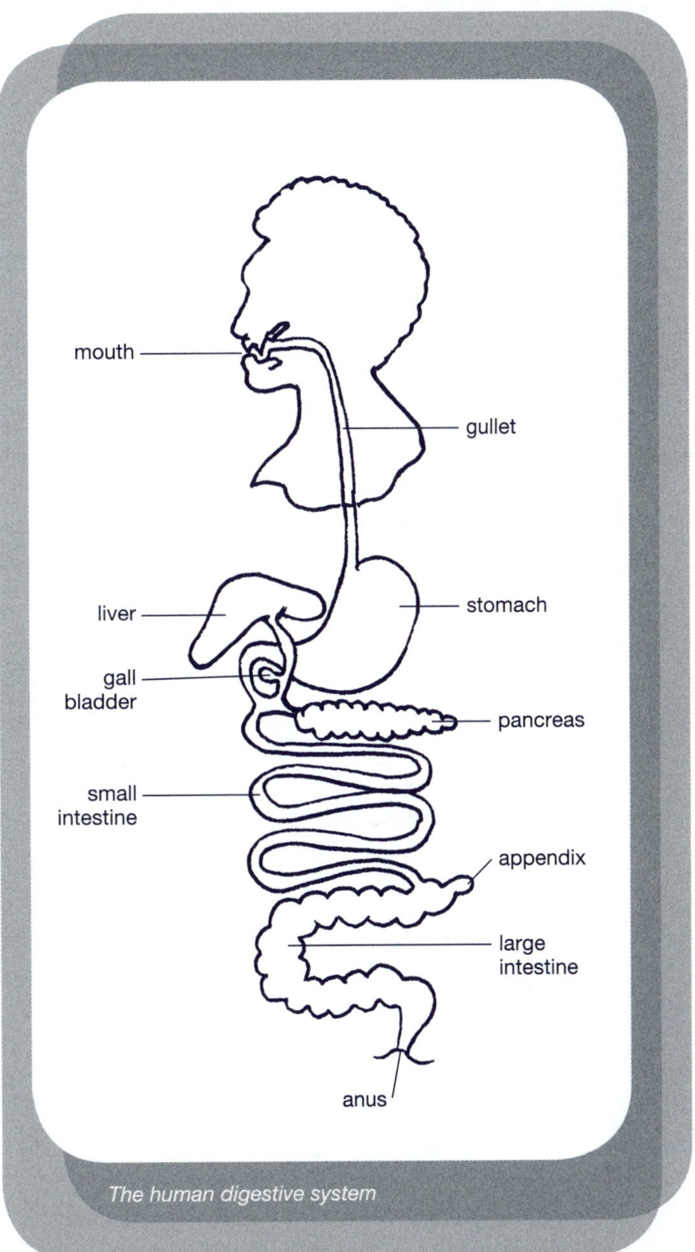

The human digestive system

food around breaking it into smaller pieces. Chemical digestion by gastric juice also occurs in the stomach. The gastric juice contains an enzyme called **protease** that breaks down complex protein into simple protein.

4 In the **small intestine** there is a little mechanical digestion and a lot of chemical digestion. The food that has been broken down passes into the blood through the wall of the small intestine.

5 In the **large intestine** water is absorbed into the bloodstream. No digestion occurs here.

6 The anus is the end of the digestive system. Undigested food is called **faeces** and passes out of the anus in a process called **elimination**.

The digestive system in humans is about 10 metres long and is folded backwards and forwards inside the body. However, the digestive system of a cow is about 25 metres long. Cows have four chambers in the stomach. One chamber stores the food that can be sent back and forth to the mouth for chewing. This extra chewing increases the mechanical digestion. Herbivores that do this are called **ruminants**. Ruminants also have bacteria in the stomach that can split open plant cells. In this way the cow can get more food from the plants that are eaten.

What happens after digestion?

- Food, mainly in the form of sugar, is carried in the blood to the cells. Cells use food energy to do their work.
- Extra food is stored in the liver or under the skin and around organs as fat.
- Fats, oils and **carbohydrates** (such as sugars and starches) are used for energy or are stored.
- Protein is needed to build new cells and repair damaged cells.
- Vitamins and minerals help the body to work.
- Water is needed to dissolve substances.

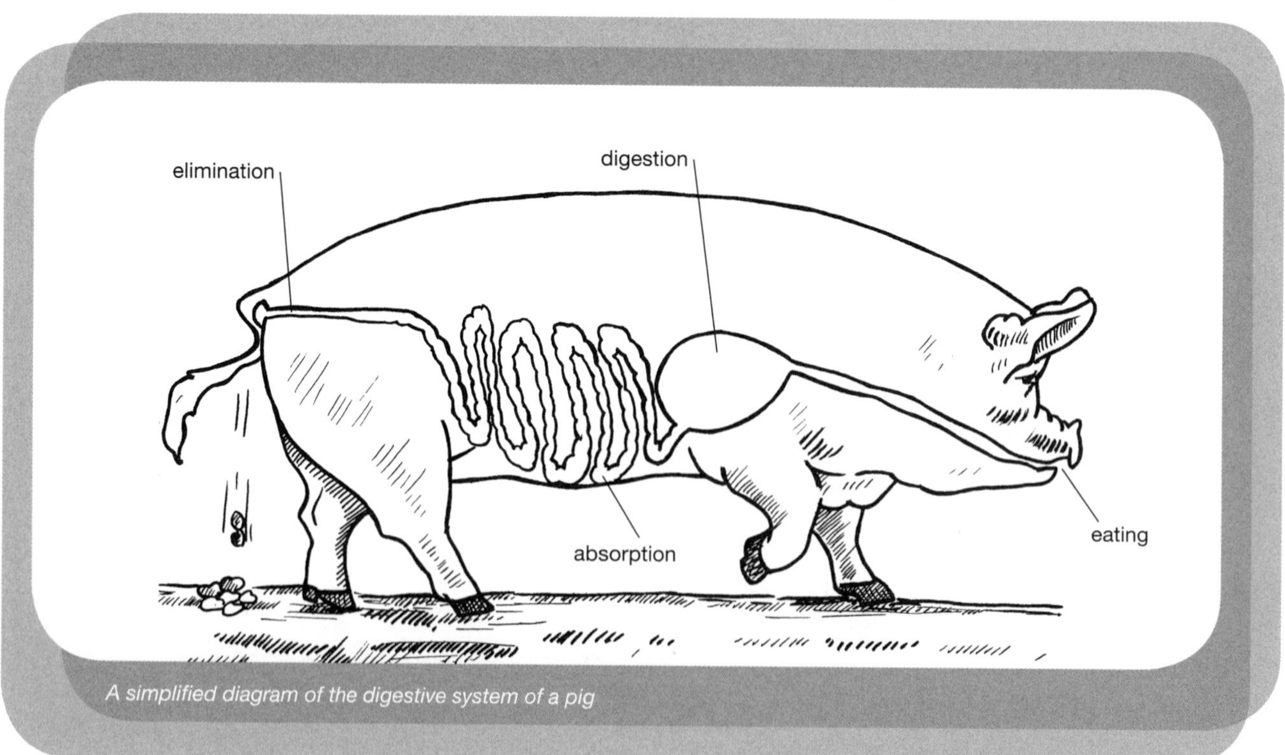

A simplified diagram of the digestive system of a pig

The table below summarises what happens to food during and after digestion:

Types of food and their digestion and use					
Food	**Essential for**	**Digested in**	**Digestive juice**	**Enzyme**	**End product**
Carbohydrates e.g. starches, sugars, cellulose	Energy	Mouth Small intestine	Saliva Pancreatic juice Intestinal juice	Amylase	Simple sugar e.g. glucose
Protein	Growth Repair Normal functioning	Stomach Small intestine	Gastric juice Pancreatic juice Intestinal juice	Protease	Amino acids
Fats and oils	Energy	Small intestine	pancreatic juice	Lipase	Fatty acids and glycerol
Vitamins	Growth Normal functioning	No digestion needed			
Mineral salts	Growth Normal functioning				
Water	Major part of body and blood Dissolving substances				

For you to try

1 **Investigation: Looking at the digestive system**

a Collect a vertebrate such as a large frog or a fish that has recently been killed, a flat container for the animal, a pair of scissors and an old newspaper.

b A chicken or pig that has been killed for eating can also be used to study the digestive system.

c Cut through the skin of the belly so you can see the organs inside.

d Carefully unfold the digestive system and try to identify the different parts of the system.

e Draw and label the different parts of the digestive system.

f Cut through the digestive tube near the mouth and near the anus and spread it out. Measure the length of the digestive system.

g Discuss your findings with other groups.

h Try to compare different animals if possible and note any similarities and differences.

i Make a poster to share your findings with others.

Ecology, relationships and interactions

Ecology is the study of how living things interact with each other and the environment. The place where an animal or plant lives is called its **habitat**. It is usually the habitat for other animals and birds as well. All the living things in one habitat are called a community. The environment is everything around a community that affects the community's way of life. Together, a community and its environment are known as an **ecosystem**.

Some of the factors that affect the environment of an organism are shown in the illustration below:

A community and the environment

When we look at the relationships between living things in a community we can see that there is a series of organisms where one feeds on the other. This feeding relationship is called a **food chain**. We can see from this relationship that all the organisms in a food chain depend on the **producer,** which is a plant. During the process of photosynthesis, plants change the energy from the Sun into food which is another type of energy. Animals are **consumers** and make use of this energy when they eat plants and when they eat other animals.

On land it is the grass and other plants that are the producers in the food chains. However, in the water tiny plants called **plankton** are the producers. There are millions of tiny plants living near the surface of the sea, lakes and ponds. Two examples of food chains that begin with plankton are shown below:

In the sea:	plankton ➔ shell fish ➔ fish ➔ man
In fresh water:	plankton ➔ mosquito larva ➔ small fish ➔ big fish

The first animal in a food chain is usually a herbivore and always eats plants. Because herbivores are the first consumers in a food chain

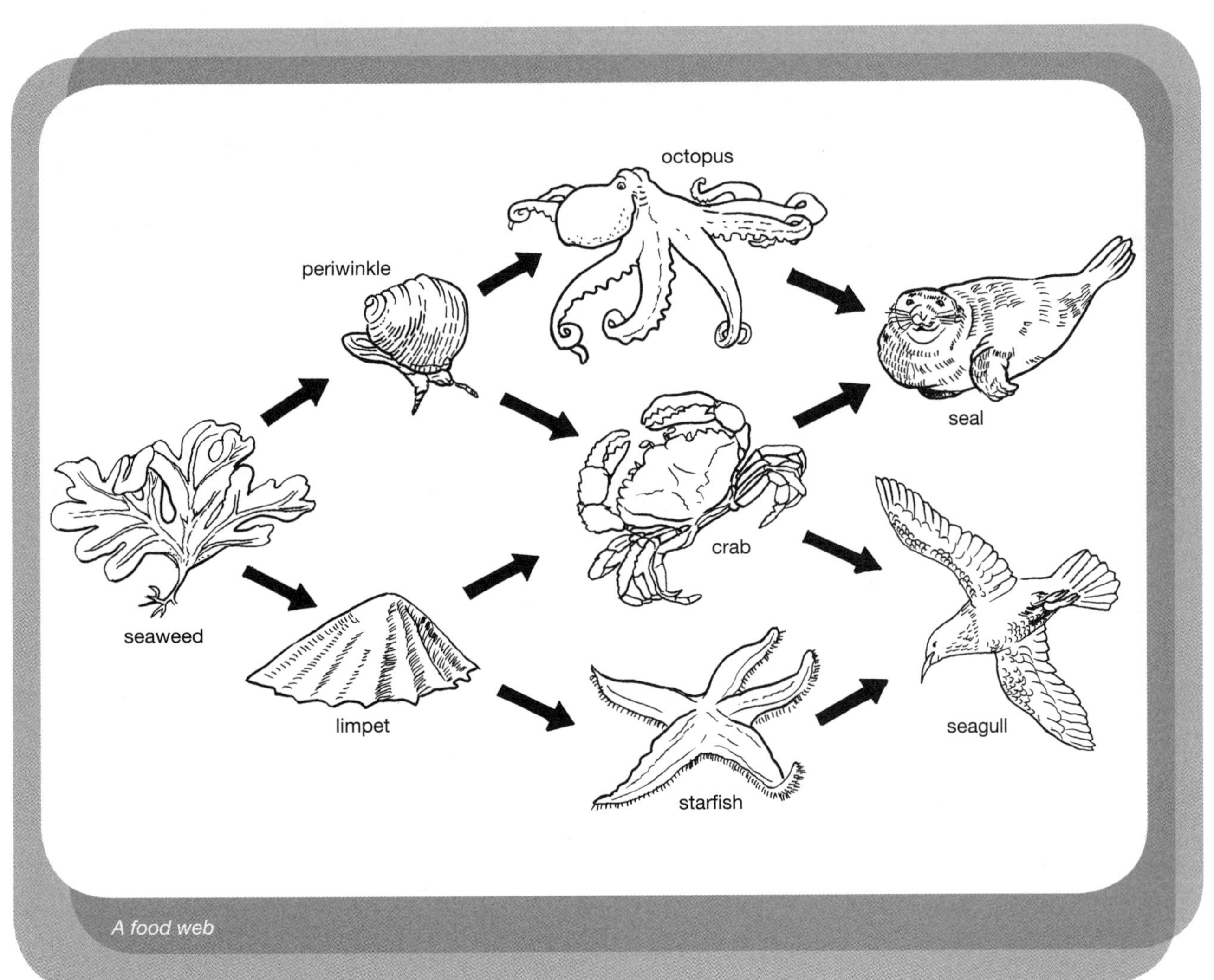

A food web

they are also called a first order consumer. The second animal in a food chain is a carnivore and usually eats herbivores. The second animal in a food chain is called a second order consumer. There may also be higher level carnivores in a food chain. Of course, animals do not eat only one kind of food, so the relationship is more complicated and is known as a **food web**. A food web is a number of food chains that are linked.

Decomposers

Decomposers are microbes such as bacteria and **fungi** that feed on the remains of dead plants and animals by making them rot or decompose. Decomposers do not take part in the food chain but they are important because

- they get rid of dead plants and animals
- they put useful chemicals back into the soil.

Materials that rot are called **biodegradable** materials. As well as dead plants and animals, biodegradable materials include things made from plants and animals such as paper, cardboard cartons, cotton, wool and leather.

For you to try

1 What is the difference between a producer and a consumer. Give an example of each.

2 What are biodegradable materials? Give two examples.

3 All people produce waste in their daily lives. Some of this waste is biodegradable and some is not. How can we best get rid of different kinds of waste materials?

4 In the food web on page 49, what other organisms would be affected if periwinkles were poisoned by chemical waste? Explain what might happen to these organisms.

5 Copy and complete the following table to show all the different names that we use for the organisms in a food chain.

Alternative names used for organisms in a food chain		
Animal →	Animal →	Animal

Pyramid of numbers

When we count the number of organisms in the different positions in a food chain we find there are fewer organisms in each position along the chain. This is because only a fraction of the energy taken in by one organism reaches the next. This means fewer and fewer organisms can be fed at each stage. For example, it might take 30 000 leaves to feed 300 snails, and 300 snails to feed one bird. This can be shown using a pyramid of numbers like the one below.

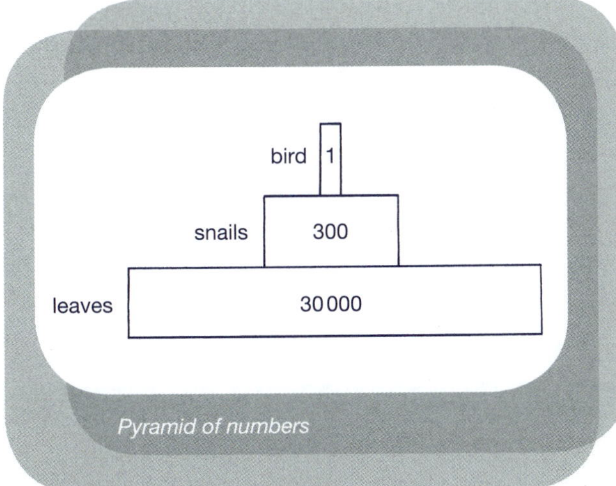

Pyramid of numbers

Pyramid of biomass

There are more organisms at the bottom of the pyramid of numbers than there are at the top. However, a leaf is lighter than a snail so the numbers of leaves and snails do not give a clear picture of how much food is being eaten at each stage of the chain.

Also, a single tree might be able to support thousands of insects, which would give a pyramid that is upside-down.

Because it is difficult to compare the numbers of organisms at each level in the food chain, scientists use the idea of **biomass**. Biomass is the total **mass** of each group of organisms. The biomass of leaves, snails and birds for the pyramid of numbers above is shown in the table below:

	A Number	B Mass of each in grams	A x B Biomass in grams
birds	1	250	250
snails	300	50	15 000
leaves	30 000	20	600 000

Using this information, a pyramid of biomass can be drawn, as shown below.

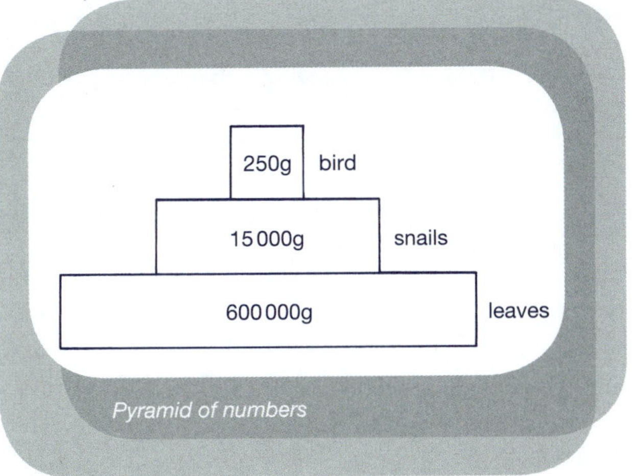

Pyramid of numbers

The pyramid of biomass is important for the food supply of humans. For example, when we look at a pyramid of biomass from the sea, it takes about one tonne of plant material to produce one kilogram of fish, such as barracuda. In the same way, when we look after pigs, it takes hundreds of kilograms of plant food like sweet potato to produce one kilogram of pork.

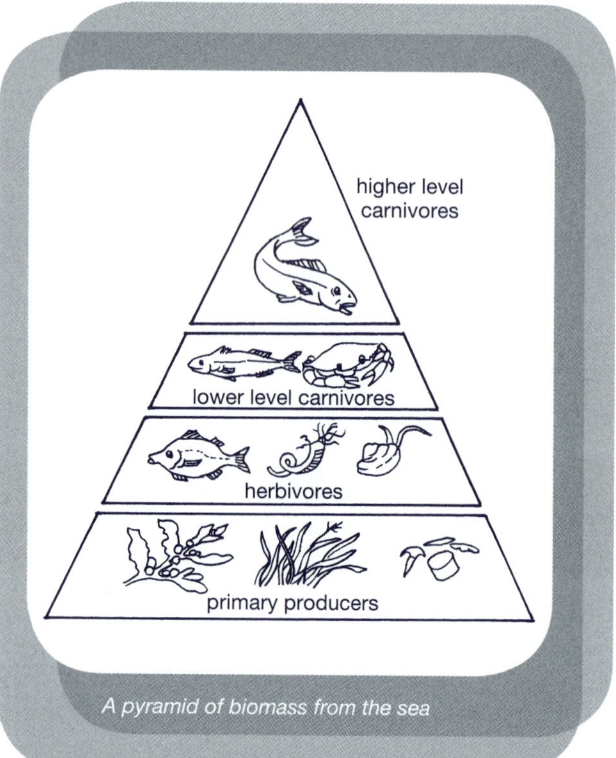

A pyramid of biomass from the sea

Energy transfer through a food chain

The pyramid of biomass shows that each animal must consume plants or other animals to obtain enough energy for its needs. It is not possible to have the same mass of higher level carnivores as lower level carnivores and herbivores. Most of the energy of the herbivores and lower level carnivores is used in the process of **respiration**, and only a little is stored in their bodies. This means that only a small amount of energy can be passed on to the next level in the food chain.

This great loss of energy along food chains explains why food chains are short. There are usually no more than four links in a chain because the amount of energy available to the top carnivore is very small.

Because it takes so much food from plants to feed animals, some people believe that we should not eat animals but only eat food that comes directly from plants. For example, **vegetarians** are people who do not eat meat or fish. **Vegans** are vegetarians who do not eat animal products like milk, butter and cheese.

For you to try

1 Look at the pyramids above, then create your own pyramids.
   - a A frog feeds on 250 worms. The worms feed on 25 000 leaves. Draw the pyramid of numbers.
   - b The frog has a mass of 200g, a worm 40g and a leaf 20g. Draw the pyramid of biomass. (Start by making a table like the one on page 51.)

2 Get into groups and discuss the following: 'Instead of growing plants to feed to chickens, pigs and cows it would be better to grow more crops to feed people.'
   - a Remember to give reasons for your point of view.
   - b Share your ideas with other groups.

Changing populations

A group of plants or animals of the same kind is called a **population**. Animals depend on plants or other animals for their food, so a change in one population may affect several other populations.

Animals that eat other animals are known as predators. The animals that predators eat are called their prey. Predators depend on their prey for food and this is called the predator–prey relationship. An animal that is a predator might also become the prey of another predator higher in the food chain.

We can understand the predator–prey relationship by looking at a garden that is a habitat for toads, slugs and plants. The toads feed on the slugs, and the slugs feed on the plants. Normally, the numbers of toads, slugs and plants will reach a balance. The graphs below show what will happen if too many toads start to develop. Over a period of time, the balance is restored.

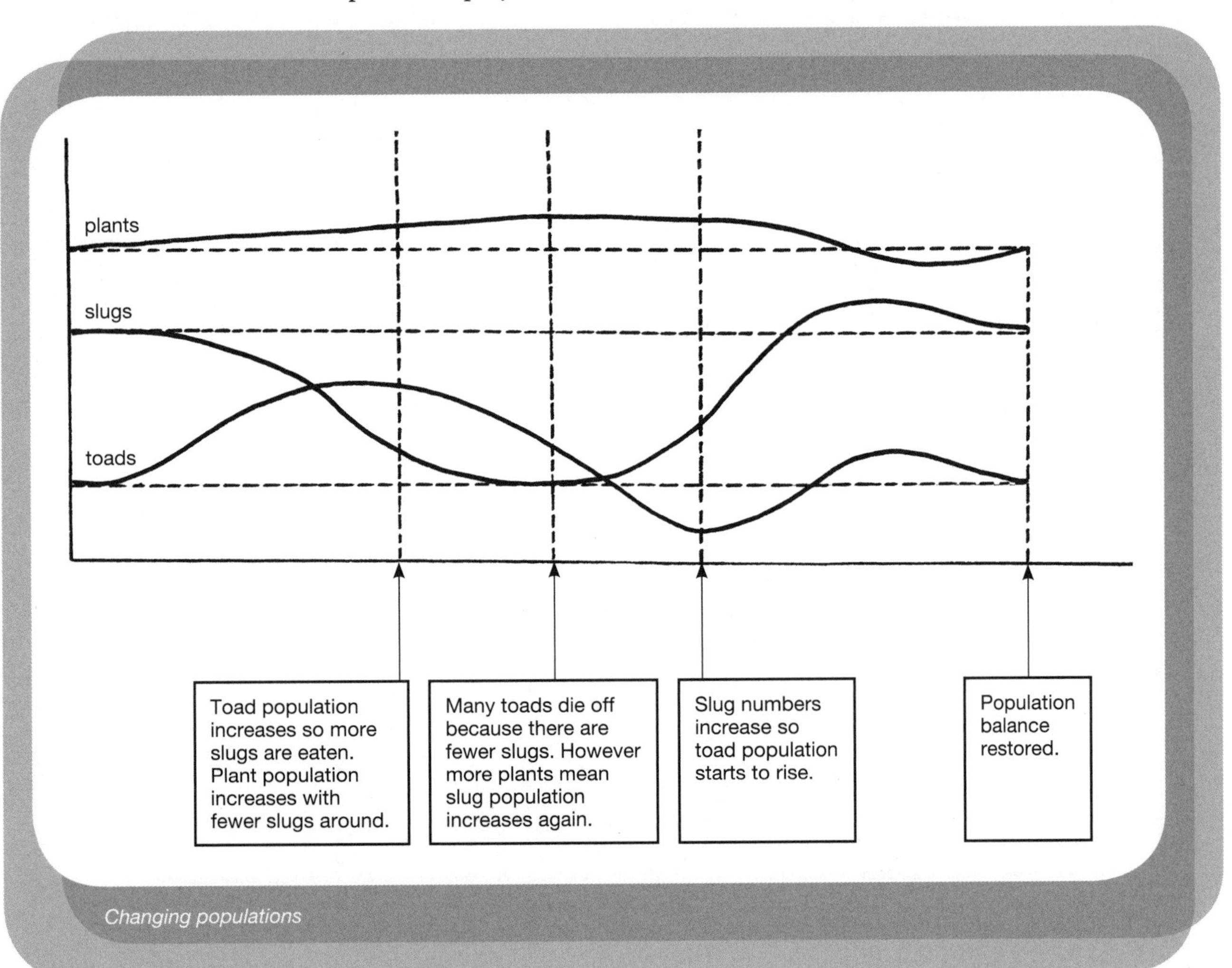

Changing populations

For you to try

1 Briefly explain why there are different numbers of living things at each level in a food pyramid.

2 **Investigation: Looking at feeding relationships**

a Go outside and observe the different living things that you can see in your area. If you live near the sea, a lake or river you can choose one of these places, but you must take care near water.

b Make a list of the plants and animals that are living together and how each obtains its food. Try to estimate the numbers of each living thing by using four groups: 'very many', 'many', 'some' and 'a few'. You could use a table like the one below.

c Draw a number of food chains to include the plants and animals that you have found.

d Identify which food chains are also predator–prey relationships. Label the predator and the prey.

e Draw a food web that includes the food chains that you have found in the area.

f Using one of the food chains you have drawn, make a pyramid of numbers for the living things that you have observed.

Name of organism	What does it feed on?	What feeds on it?	Estimate of numbers			
			Very many	Many	Some	A few

Competition

Competition occurs when organisms need the same **resource** and there is a limited amount of it. Plants or animals that do not get enough of the available resources will become weak or die. For example, the weeds growing in a garden will prevent the crops from getting nutrients from the soil. Pulling out the weeds will remove the competition and the crops will grow well.

Farmers can also help to solve the problem of competition by removing the weaker looking plants. This practice is called **thinning** and means that the remaining plants get more nutrients and grow better.

Many animals are competing for food, water, nesting places, shelter and other resources. Some animals establish territories to make sure they have enough resources. A territory is an area that is defended against other animals. For example, many birds sing in the early morning and evening to warn other birds that this is their territory.

competition

no competition

The effect of weeds on the growth of corn

Birds establish territories to make sure they have enough food.

Using our environment wisely

The lessons that we learn from ecology can be used to help communities manage their environments wisely. For example, we know that natural environments are stable and easier to manage because they are **diverse**, which means that they contain many different types of living things.

People have traditionally managed their environment wisely in Papua New Guinea. For example, traditional methods of catching fish did not remove large amounts of fish. However, commercial fishing boats are now catching large numbers of fish and careful management is necessary so that the fish can reproduce.

People have used the forest to make gardens and as a source of building materials, firewood and medicine, as well as for hunting. However, because of logging, forests are now being cut down faster than they are regrowing. In some places **clear felling** means that all the trees have been cut down. This results in soil **erosion** and makes it difficult for the trees to regenerate. Forests should undergo **selective logging** so that only certain types of trees and of a certain size are cut down.

With modern farming methods, usually only one kind of crop is grown at a time. This means that the crop can easily be attacked by a disease or eaten by insect pests or other animals. Because there is little diversity this system of farming is unstable. Subsistence farmers do not usually have this problem because they grow different crops together on the same piece of land.

Another problem of modern farming is the use of chemical **fertilisers** to make plants grow better, and **pesticides** to kill insects and other pests. These chemicals can poison people and other animals, especially when they get into water or get into the food chain. Farmers also find that, after some time, pesticides do not always work so well.

Many of the lessons that we learn from ecology also apply to humans. A bigger population means that we need more food, clean water and air, as well as sufficient clothing, shelter and **fuel**. A larger population also needs more services such as schools and hospitals. Many countries, including Papua New Guinea, are finding it hard to provide enough for their increasing population.

The cane toad is a pest found all over Papua New Guinea.

For you to try

1 What is competition? What are the advantages and disadvantages of competition?
2 Choose one example of human activity that has an impact on the environment. For example, over-hunting, over-fishing, logging, introduced species like the cane toad, and the use of chemical fertilisers or pesticides.

Choose a topic from one of the above examples so that one team will support the topic and one team will be against the topic. Each team should prepare their ideas and then the two teams can have a debate.

Summary questions

1 Copy the table below and match the sentences on the left with the correct words on the right.

A	The green material in leaves.	**I**	roots
B	Plants make food in these.	**II**	water
C	The largest group of plants.	**III**	spores
D	Plants that have needle-like leaves and cones.	**IV**	chlorophyll
E	Ferns reproduce using these.	**V**	flowering plants
F	Seaweed belongs to this group of plants.	**VI**	leaves
G	Needed for plants to live.	**VII**	photosynthesis
H	The process by which plants make food.	**VIII**	mangrove
I	Hold the plant in the ground.	**IX**	conifers
J	A tree that can grow in water and has breathing roots	**X**	algae

2 Animals without a backbone are called

A vertebrates

B amphibians

C mammals

D invertebrates

3 An animal with a scaly skin lives on the land and reproduces by laying eggs. It is most likely

A an amphibian

B a bird

C a monotreme

D a reptile

4 We can tell mammals from other animals because they all have

A a backbone

B fur or hair

C cold blood

D young that are born alive

5 Which of the following best describes the characteristics that help an animal to live in its environment?

I the general structure of the animal

II the body covering

III the digestive system

A I only

B II only

C I and II only

D I, II and III

6 Which of the following body coverings best match the environment in which the animal lives?

Environment in which animal lives	Body covering of animal
A Lives on the land, some can swim or dive, most can fly	**I** Dry, scaly skin of reptile
B Usually lives on the land producing live young	**II** Scales of fish
C Always lives in water	**III** Moist skin of amphibian, may be rough or smooth
D Usually lives on land, some can live in water	**IV** Fur of mammals
E Can live on land or in water but usually needs to be near water, especially to reproduce	**V** Feathers of birds

7 Use the following key to identify the three fish shown below.

1	**a** **b**	more than 50 cm long ➔ less than 50 cm long ➔	go to 2 ➔ go to 4 ➔
2	**a** **b**	has round head and jaw ➔ has V-shaped head and pointed jaw ➔	go to 3 ➔ Saurichthys
3	**a** **b**	has large scales ➔ has small scales ➔	Colobodus Birgeria
4	**a** **b**	more than 10 cm long ➔ less than 10 cm long ➔	go to 5 ➔ Peltopleurus
5	**a** **b**	broad, flat body shape ➔ long, smooth body shape ➔	Bobasatrania Ptycholepsis

8 Which of the following best describes the correct sequence of movement of food through the human digestive system?

A gullet ➔ intestines ➔ stomach ➔ anus

B mouth ➔ gullet ➔ stomach ➔ intestines

C mouth ➔ stomach ➔ gullet ➔ anus

D mouth ➔ stomach ➔ gullet ➔ intestines

9 Which of the following best describe the importance of decomposers in an ecosystem?

I They take part in every food chain

II They get rid of dead plants and animals

III They put useful chemicals back into the soil

A I and II only

B I and III

C II and III only

D I, II and III

10 Which of the following statements about biomass are true?

I The numbers of living things give a clear picture of how much food is being eaten at each stage of the chain.

II It is difficult to compare the numbers of organisms at each level in the food chain.

III Biomass is the total mass of each group of organisms in a food chain.

A I and II only

B II and III only

C I and III only

D I, II and III

11 Which of the following is most likely to be the best description of a predator in a food chain?

A a herbivore

B a carnivore

C a top carnivore

D an omnivore

12 Which of the following human activities are most likely to cause the biggest problems for the environment in Papua New Guinea?

A subsistence agriculture, making roads, using firewood

B use of chemical fertilisers, collecting rubbish, burning off a garden

C planting cash crops, getting rid of introduced species like the cane toad, clear-felling

D logging, commercial fishing with nets, use of chemical pesticides.

13 The passage below is a summary of the main ideas of this chapter. Copy and complete the passage in your book. Using the words in the list, find the words that are missing. You can use each word only once.

activities, body, digestive, energy, environment, feeding, food, job, relationship, structures, system

The structure of living things helps them to live in the ______________. The different ______________ of living things allow them to live in different environments.

The structure of the different parts of living things is related to the ______________ which the part must do. All animals have a ______________ covering that is suited to the place where it lives. The ______________ system of humans allows them break down food that we eat.

Breaking down food provides us with ______________ and also produces waste.

Other animals also have a digestive ______________. The type of digestive system depends on the kind of ______________ that the animal eats.

The plants and animals living together in an ecosystem are in a ______________ relationship called a food web. Human beings are also part of a food web and have a ______________ with other plants and animals in the environment. The ______________ of humans have a bigger effect on the environment than any other animal because of the way we obtain food and use other resources.

3

Science in the home

Chapter summary

In this chapter you will have an opportunity to:

- find out how matter is made and the way it behaves
- find out about the properties of materials before and after changes take place
- find out how energy can change from one form to another
- find out and share ideas about simple machines and how they can be used in homes and the community to make life easier.

Syllabus references

Strand: Science in the home

Sub-strands: Learning about substances

Using energy in the home

Outcomes:

7.3.1 Explain the structure of matter in terms of the particles from which it is made

7.3.2 Compare the properties of materials before and after physical and chemical changes and identify patterns in the types of changes that take place in the materials used

7.3.3 Investigate how energy changes from one form to another

7.3.4 Investigate how we use force in everyday life

7.3.5 Identify and make recommendations on how simple machines can make life easier through community field study

Key facts

- Everything is made of matter and all matter is made of tiny particles.
- The way that particles are arranged in different kinds of matter affects the properties of the matter or the way that the matter behaves.
- Matter can change and when it changes it will have different properties.
- When matter changes, the change can be a physical change or a chemical change.
- Physical changes are usually reversible and no new substances are formed. A change of state is an example of a physical change.
- Chemical changes are usually not reversible and new substances are formed. Burning is an example of a chemical change.
- Energy can exist in many different forms such as heat, light and sound.
- Energy can change from one form to another.
- Friction has advantages and disadvantages.
- Forces can be used in everyday life to make things move, to slow them down and to speed them up.
- Simple machines can do work and make life easier.

Learning about substances

States of matter

Everything around us is made of **matter** and we use many different types of matter every day. Whenever we use something we are using different **states** of matter because matter must always be a **solid**, **liquid** or **gas**. For example, we use solid timber to make a fence to keep pigs out of the garden, we use water to wash our clothes because it is liquid, and we blow air into a balloon because the air is a gas and it will help the balloon to float. We could fill the balloon with water, but then it would not float.

All solids, liquids and gases are made up of tiny **particles** and scientists can explain how they behave using the particle model of matter.

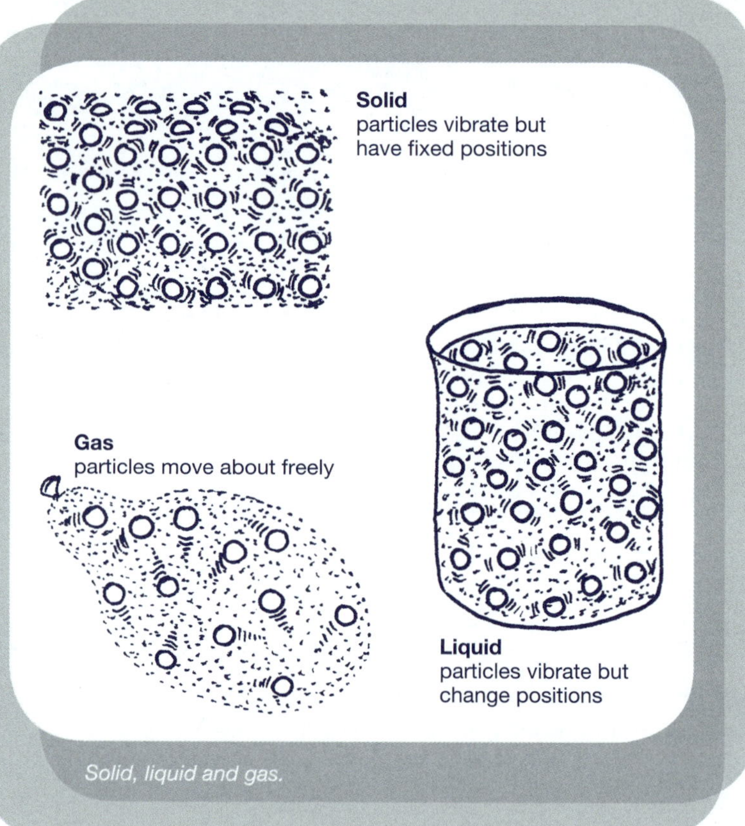

Solid, liquid and gas.

In a solid the particles are held together by strong **forces** of attraction. The particles vibrate from side to side, but they cannot change positions. So a solid has a fixed size and shape.

In a liquid the particles are still pulled together by forces of attraction but strong **vibrations** mean that the particles have enough energy to change position and move past each other. This means that the liquid can flow and take up the shape of the container.

In a gas the particles are spaced out and there is very little attraction between them. The particles move about at high speed and quickly fill the space available. A gas has no fixed size or shape.

For you to try

1 Copy and complete the following table to show the different types of matter that you use every day and the way in which you use it.

Matter that is used every day		
Solids	**Liquids**	**Gases**

2 **Investigation: Making a gas**

a Collect a small glass bottle, some bicarbonate of soda, some vinegar, a balloon and a small candle (a candle that is only a few centimetres high is best).

b Pour about five tablespoons of vinegar into the small glass bottle.

c Pour half a tablespoon of bicarbonate of soda down a folded piece of paper or card into the glass bottle.

d Quickly put the balloon onto the neck of the bottle.

e Observe what happens.

f The gas that is produced is called carbon dioxide.

g Remove the balloon from the neck of the bottle.

h Light the candle and slowly and carefully pour the gas from the bottle onto the candle. You will need to hold the bottle almost horizontal so that the vinegar and bicarbonate of soda stay inside the bottle.

i Observe what happens.

j Write a scientific report of your investigation to explain what you did and what you found out.

3 Compare the behaviour of the particles. What differences are there between the particles in

a a solid and a liquid

b a liquid and a gas?

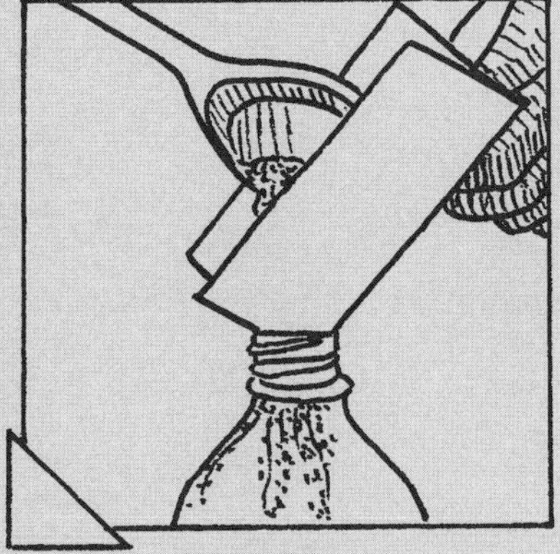

Properties of materials

The characteristics of a material and how it behaves are called its **properties**. Some of the words used to describe the properties of different materials are shown in the table to the right.

Property	Meaning	Example
Strong	Resists the effects of forces	Steel
Brittle	Hard, but breaks easily	Glass
Malleable	Can be hammered into shape	Copper
Ductile	Can be pulled out into wires	Copper
Transparent	'See-through' or lets light through	White polythene
Opaque	Lets light through, but scatters it	White polythene
Conductor (heat)	Lets heat pass through easily	Copper
Conductor (electricity)	Lets electricity pass through easily	Copper
Insulator (heat)	Stops heat passing through	Expanded polystyrene
Insulator (electricity)	Stops electricity passing through	PVC

Grouping solids

There are different ways of putting solids into groups. For example, the materials that are used for making things that we use in every day life can be put into five groups:

Pottery or *ceramics* **Brittle** materials made by heating clay. They can usually stand high temperatures.

Glasses Brittle materials, made partly from sand. They are **transparent** or **opaque**, and are good electrical **insulators**.

Materials used in everyday things

Plastics Made from chemicals (synthetic). Can be moulded into shapes. Often flexible when cold. Melt easily. Good electrical insulators.

Metals **Metals** are shiny solids that conduct heat and electricity. They are often **malleable** and **ductile** and difficult to melt.

Fibres Threads made from natural or synthetic materials and used to make bilums and fabrics.

Metals and alloys

Metals are useful because of their properties. Most metals are hard solids that can be flattened into sheets and stretched into wire. For example, aluminium is used in cooking pots, copper in wires and lead in car batteries. Sometimes two metals are joined because of their properties. For example, most food cans are made of iron covered with a layer of tin. Sheets of iron coated with a layer of zinc are used as galvanised iron for roofing and water tanks. In both cases the iron is protected from rusting.

However, most metals are not used in their **pure** state. Mixing different metals to form **alloys** can produce a metal with special properties.

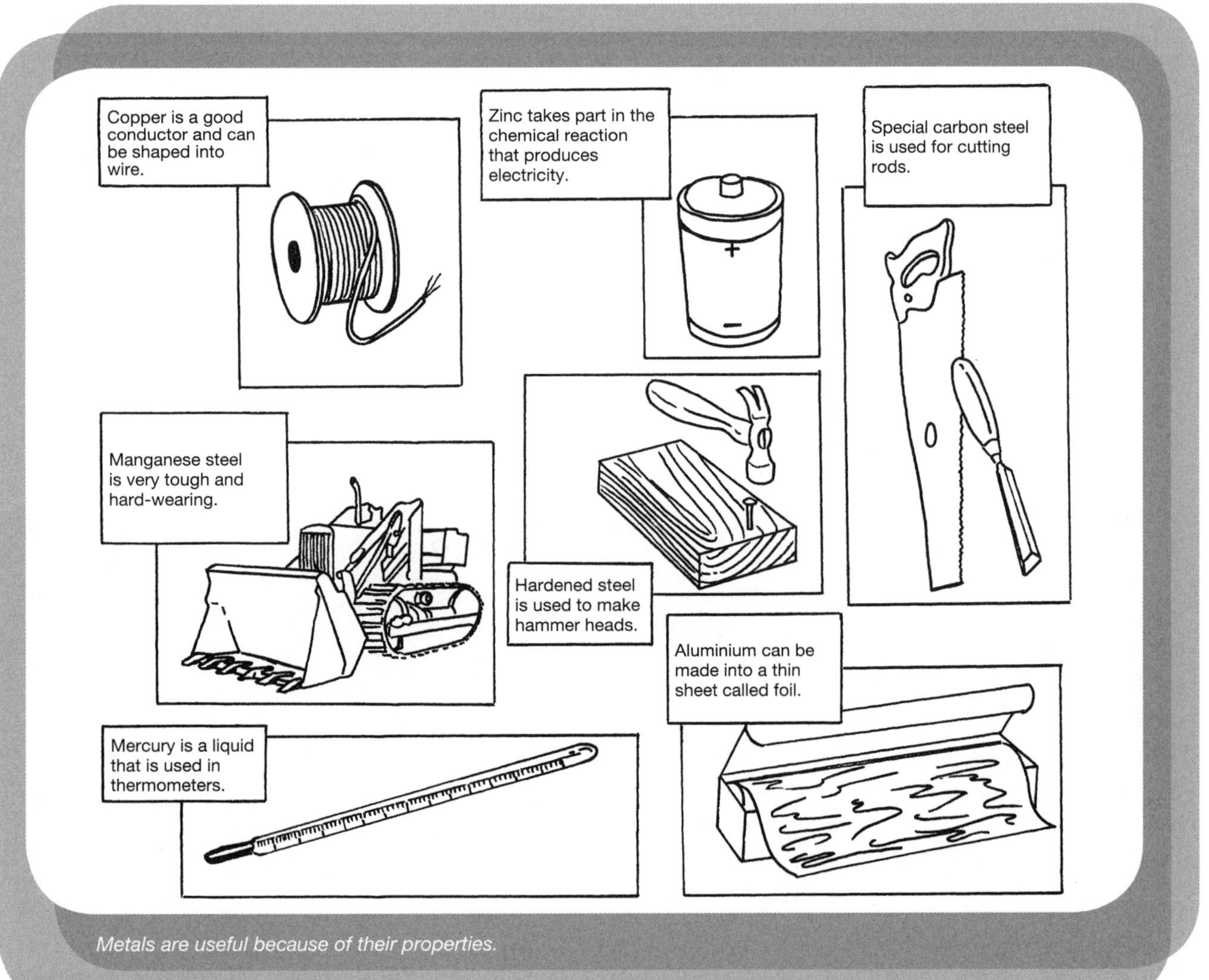

Metals are useful because of their properties.

Some common alloys are shown in the table:

Alloy	Metals contained in the alloy	Properties	Uses
brass	copper and zinc	easy to cast, does not corrode	taps, bullet cases
solder	lead and tin	melts easily	join metals in tanks, gutters, wires
bronze	copper and tin	easy to cast, does not corrode	boat fittings, statues
stainless steel	iron, chromium, manganese, nickel	strong and hard; does not corrode	knives, forks, spoons, saucepans, sinks, bolts, wire

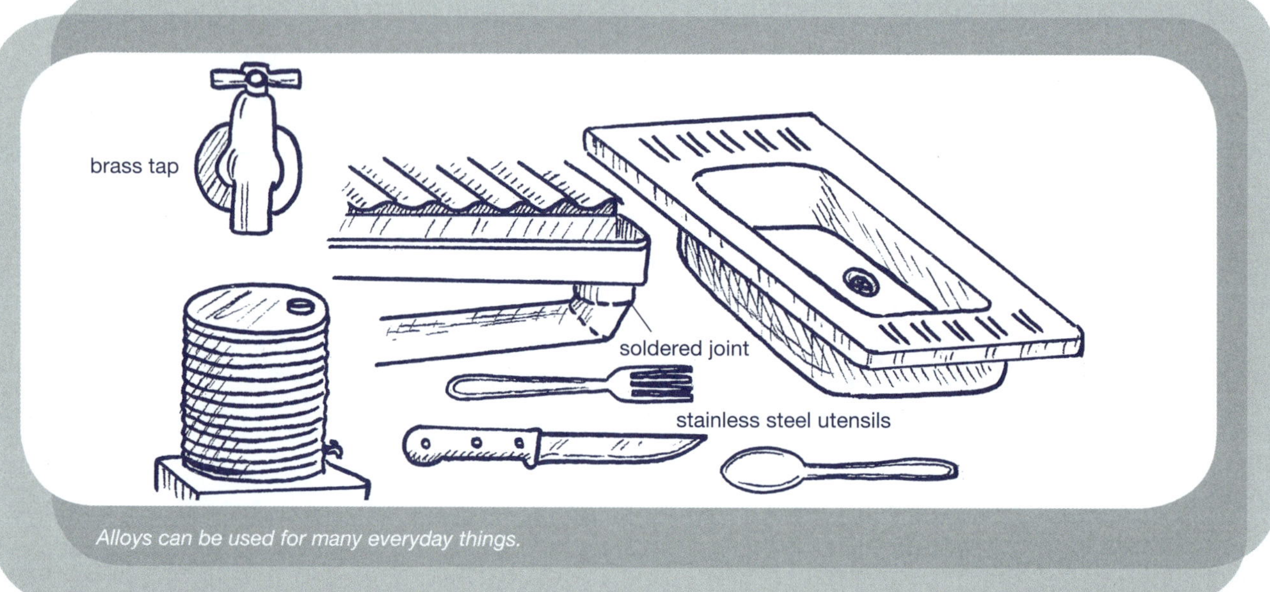

Alloys can be used for many everyday things.

For you to try

1 Collect a variety of different materials and classify them according to their physical properties. Remember that materials can have more than one property.

2 Look at the list below of jobs to be done by different materials. What properties should each material have?'

- **a** a knife
- **b** the handle of a kettle
- **c** the bottom of a saucepan
- **d** the covering of an electric wire
- **e** the window of a bathroom or toilet.

3 Make a list of the metal objects that you have used today. Which of these were alloys? What metals did the alloys contain? One way of doing this would be to put the information in a table.

Changing matter

Everything in the world is made of **matter**. Air, water, soil, plants and animals are all made of matter. However, matter does not always stay the same but can change over time. For example:

- water boils to form a gas and freezes to form ice
- wood is burned to provide heat energy
- iron joins with other matter in the air to form rust
- an electric current makes the wire filament in a lamp glow and give off light energy
- dead animals and plants decay or decompose.

Many changes to matter, such as the rusting of iron, the ripening of fruit and the **evaporation** of water, take place naturally.

People also make many changes to matter. They take naturally occurring materials, called **raw materials**, and change them into new useful substances, called **products**.

For a long time people have been able to change substances, such as limestone into lime or iron ore into iron. They have learned to extract useful substances, such as oil from coconuts or salt from seawater, and make glass from sand.

People now know how to make very complicated changes to matter, such as the manufacture of medicine and plastics from petroleum, which is found under the ground.

When matter changes it can be a **physical change** or a **chemical change**.

Bilums can be made from nylon.

Glass is made from sand.

Paper is made from wood.

Physical changes

When matter changes but no new substance is formed, it is called a physical change. For example, when you sharpen your pencil you have made a physical change. You have changed some of the wood and graphite into shavings and powder but you have not made any new substances. Other examples of physical changes are:

- chopping wood
- making sago
- dissolving sugar in tea or coffee
- sharpening a grass knife
- tearing up a piece of paper
- the erosion of soil after heavy rain
- clothes or a pair of thongs wearing out.

Many physical changes are useful but some are not, and might be a problem.

When tyres wear out, this is a physical change.

Running water can wear away rocks into soil and sand.

For you to try

1 Copy and complete the following table to show physical changes that are useful and those that are not useful, or that may be a problem:

Physical changes that are useful	Physical changes that are not useful

Types of physical changes

Physical changes include:

1 changes of state
2 dissolving
3 making and separating **mixtures**.

1 Changes of state

The three states of matter are solid, liquid and gas. When matter changes state, a physical change takes place.

Water is a good example of a substance that can change state easily. When water is cooled it can change to ice. This is known as **freezing** or **solidification**. Cooling is the removal of heat.

When water is heated it can change state into a colourless gas called steam. This is known as **boiling**. Steam and ice are different forms of water and no new substances have been formed. When steam is cooled it can change into liquid water. This change is called **condensation**. When ice is heated it will change into liquid water. Again, no new substances are formed. These changes of state of water occur at two fixed temperatures. The change from solid to liquid occurs at 0° C which is known at the melting point or freezing point. The change from liquid to gas occurs at 100°C which is known as the boiling point.

Liquid water can also change to a gas at a lower temperature than the boiling point. For example, when a puddle dries up after rain or when wet clothes are hanging on the line to dry. This process is known as evaporation.

Heat must be added or removed from a substance for a change of state to take place. Heat is added to bring about melting and evaporation. Heat is

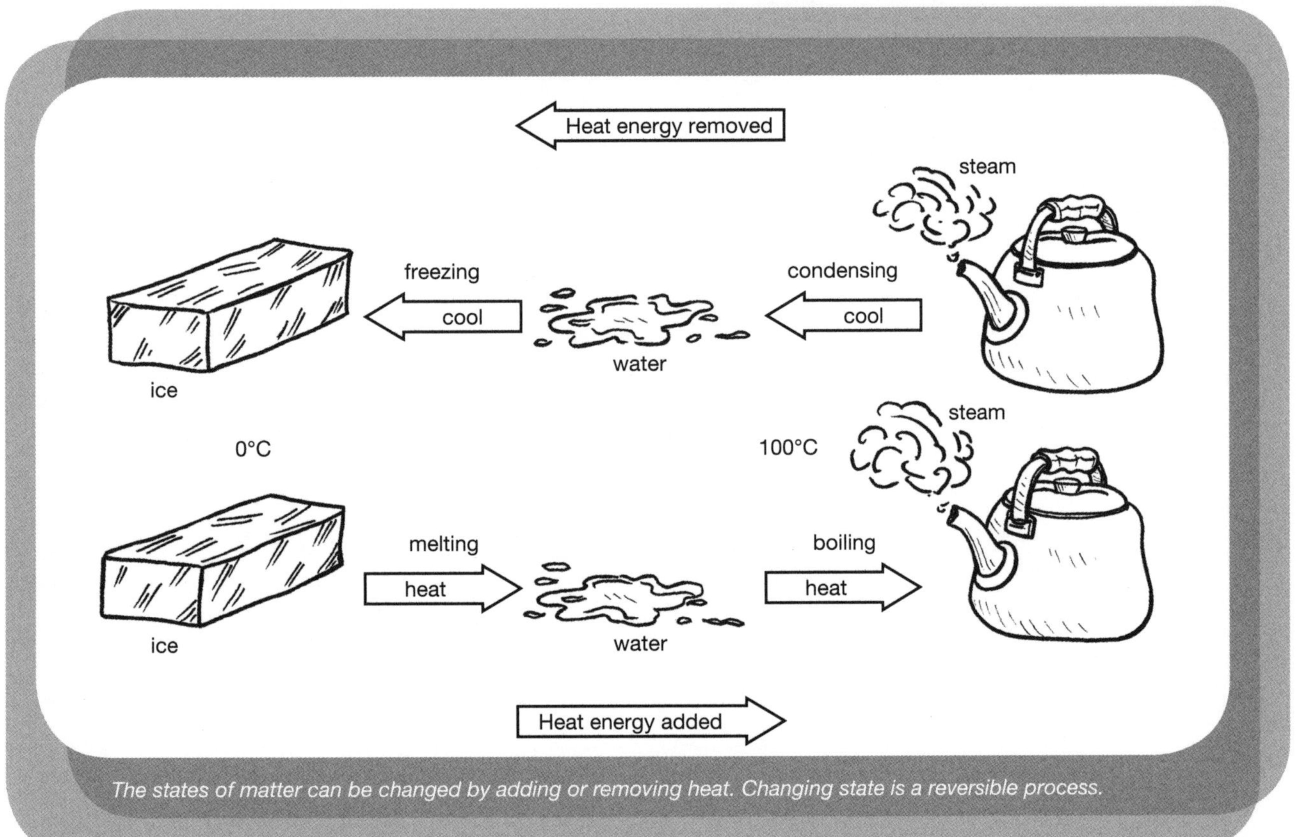

The states of matter can be changed by adding or removing heat. Changing state is a reversible process.

removed to bring about condensation or freezing. These changes are shown in the diagram below.

Many other substances also change state. For example, when metals such as lead, iron and gold are heated to a high temperature they become liquids and can be poured into **moulds**. When they cool they become solid again. The process of pouring liquid metal into a mould is also known as **casting** and is used to make objects with different shapes. Engines are made from many different shaped pieces called castings.

Pouring molten gold. Gold melts at 1064°C.

Particles and change of state

All matter is made of particles called **atoms** that are always moving. When matter is heated, the particles gain energy, and when matter is cooled, the particles lose energy.

In the solid state, the particles of matter are packed close together. They have little energy and can only vibrate. This means that the particles can only move forwards and backwards in about the same position.

When a solid is heated, the particles gain energy and can move more. Eventually, the particles have enough energy to move around, but they still stay close together. This results in the solid melting, and a liquid is formed.

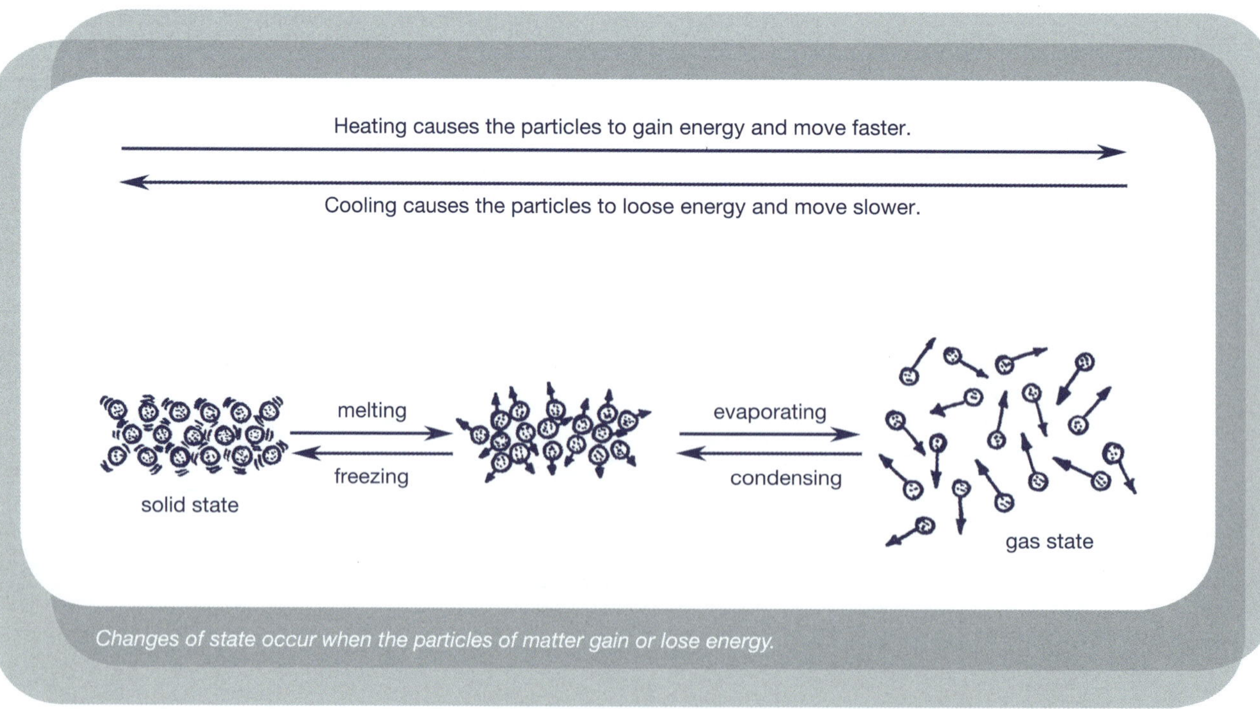

Changes of state occur when the particles of matter gain or lose energy.

For you to try

1 Collect local materials such as clay, stones, and the seeds of plants. In groups, use the materials to make a simple model to show the particle structure of a solid. Label your model and display it to the other groups in the class.

2 Make a poster to show the particle structure of a solid, liquid and gas. Label your poster.

3 Copy and complete the table below to show what happens when matter changes state. The first example has been completed for you.

Changing state			
Change of state	**Name of change**	**Change in energy**	**Change to particle movement**
Solid to liquid	Melting	Energy gained	Move more freely
Gas to liquid			
Liquid to gas			
Liquid to solid			

When a liquid is heated, the particles gain energy and move more. If enough energy is supplied the particles break away from each other and form a gas. In the gas state the particles move at high speeds and are far apart from each other.

When heat is removed, the movement of the particles slows down and they come closer together. When cooled, a gas will condense to form a liquid, and a liquid will freeze or solidify to form a solid.

The changes that happen to the particles during a physical change, such as a change of state, can be shown in a diagram. The particles themselves do not change but are arranged differently.

Dissolving

When we put substances such as salt and sugar into water, they dissolve and disappear. When salt dissolves in water, the large crystals of salt break up into particles. The particles of salt mix with the particles of water, and you cannot see the salt because the particles are so small.

There are spaces between the water particles into which the salt particles fit. Stirring helps the large salt crystals break up into particles and speeds up the process of dissolving.

Substances that dissolve are described as **soluble**. Substances that do not dissolve are described as **insoluble**.

The substance that dissolves is called the **solute**. The substance that does the dissolving is called the **solvent**.

Dissolving is a physical change because no new substances are formed. The particles of the solute and solvent are simply mixed together. You can observe this by sipping the salt water—you cannot see the salt particles but you know they are there because you can taste them.

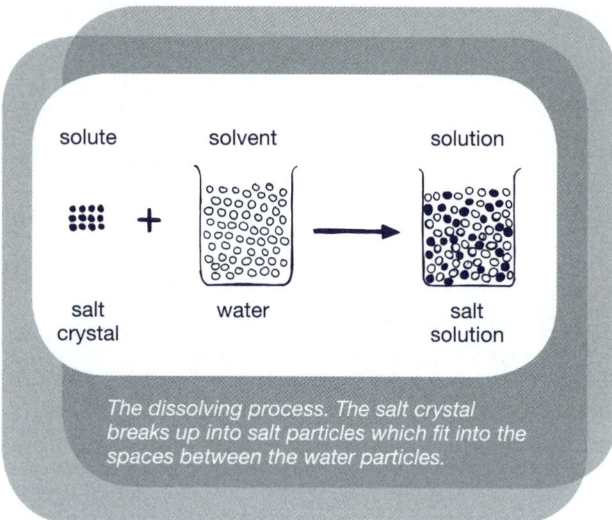

The dissolving process. The salt crystal breaks up into salt particles which fit into the spaces between the water particles.

Saturated solutions

When we add a small amount of salt or sugar to water in a glass and stir the water, it dissolves to form a weak solution, which we can taste. When we add a lot of salt or sugar to water, it dissolves to form a strong solution, and we can taste the difference. If we keep adding more salt or sugar to the water then we reach a point where no more solute will dissolve even if we keep stirring. The solution at this stage is called a **saturated solution** because no more solute can be dissolved. However, when a saturated solution is heated, the solid material in the bottom dissolves.

Separating mixtures

Many of the things around us contain more than one substance and are called mixtures. For example, air is a mixture of gases such as oxygen, nitrogen, carbon dioxide and others. Soil, cordial, milk, blood and sea water are also mixtures.

When two substances are mixed together, the particles of the two substances do not change. Each of the two substances keeps its own properties and can be separated by a physical process such as decanting or dissolving and filtering.

For you to try

1 **Investigation: The effect of heat when dissolving solutes**
   - a Collect a small glass jar, some salt, some sugar, cold water and hot water, and a teaspoon.
   - b Put a small amount of cold water in the jar. Put a mark on the jar to show the level of the water.
   - c Use the teaspoon to add salt to the water and stir.
   - d Continue to add salt and stir until no more salt will dissolve. Record the number of teaspoons of salt that you have added.
   - e Repeat using the same amount of hot water and again record the number of teaspoons of salt that you have added.
   - f Repeat the experiment using sugar instead of salt, but again using cold water and hot water.
   - g Write up a scientific report of your investigation to describe what you did and what you have found out.

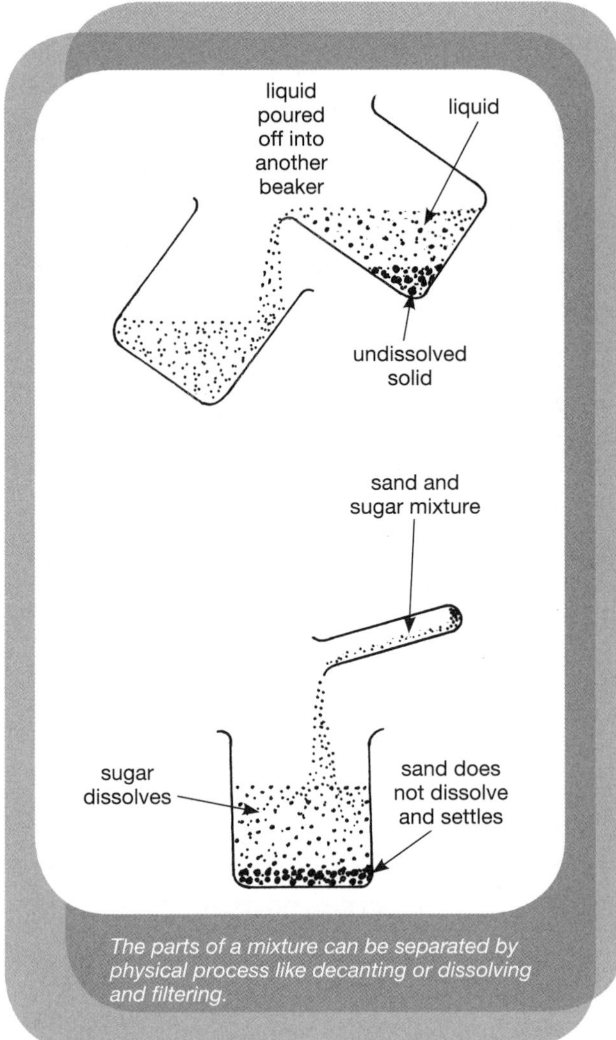

The parts of a mixture can be separated by physical process like decanting or dissolving and filtering.

Separating iron and sulphur

The simplest kind of matter that can exist is called an **element**. Pure iron is an element and is made up of particles of iron. Pure sulphur is also an element and is made up of particles of sulphur. When we put some yellow sulphur and grey iron filings together, they mix with each other but no new substances are formed. The iron and sulphur form a mixture and this mixing is a physical change.

The mixture contains iron particles and sulphur particles mixed, but not joined, together. If the particles joined together they would form new substances.

The iron can be separated from the sulphur by using a **magnet** and the yellow sulphur will be left behind. The separation of iron and sulphur in this way is an example of a physical change.

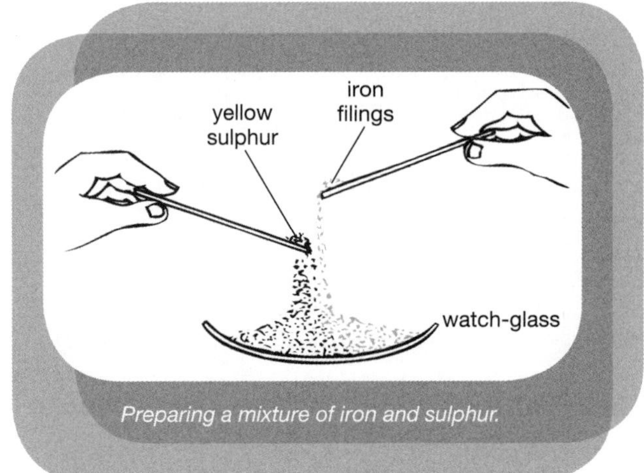

Preparing a mixture of iron and sulphur.

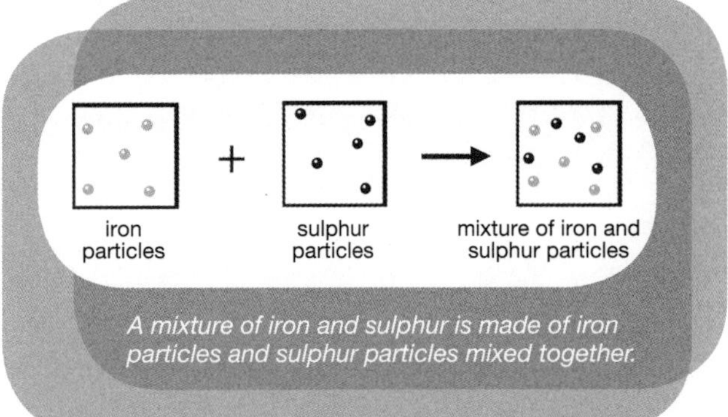

A mixture of iron and sulphur is made of iron particles and sulphur particles mixed together.

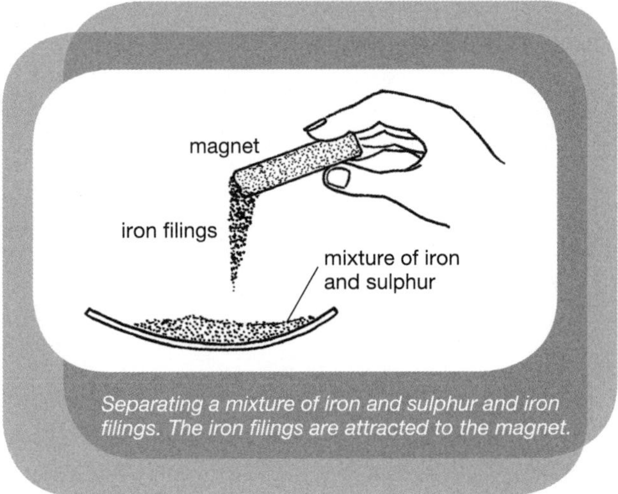

Separating a mixture of iron and sulphur and iron filings. The iron filings are attracted to the magnet.

Distillation

When a solute dissolves in a solvent a mixture called a **solution** is formed. No new substances are formed in the solution and this is an example of a physical change. The mixture can be separated using a process called **distillation**. For example, sea water is a mixture. Water is the solvent and the salts that are dissolved in it are the solutes. Heat energy is used to make the water evaporate leaving behind the salts. When the water vapour is cooled, it will change state again and produce distilled water, which is pure water that does not contain any salt. Removing salt from water by distillation is also called **desalination**.

Distillation or desalination can be used to obtain fresh water from sea water using a **solar still**. A solar still can be made from a shallow pan of salt water covered by a sloping sheet of glass or plastic. The rays of the sun pass through the glass and evaporate the water. The water vapour condenses on the underside of the glass and trickles down the sloping surface and is collected in a trough.

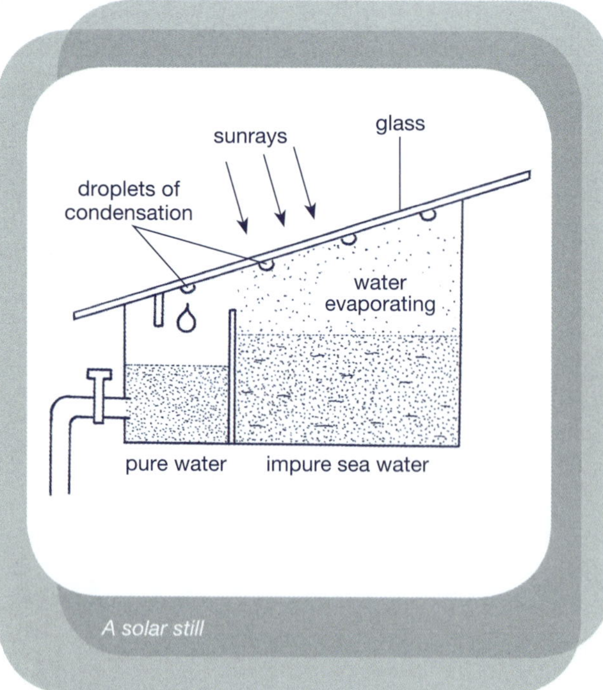

A solar still

This kind of solar still can produce about one litre of fresh water from 10 litres of sea water per day.

For you to try

1. What is meant by a 'physical change'?
2. What has to be done to a substance before it changes state?
3. Give three examples of physical changes that you make to matter every day.
4. Explain why each of the following situations involves a physical change.
   a. wet clothes drying on a line
   b. scraping and squeezing coconut
   c. putting some sugar in hot water.
5. Imagine that you and three friends are stuck on an island in the sea for a week and you each need one litre of fresh water every day to survive. Using the information above, you each make a solar still. How many litres of sea water will you and your friends use altogether in order to obtain enough fresh water?

Chemical changes

When matter changes and new substances are formed a chemical change has taken place. For example:

- when we light a fire the wood burns to give heat, smoke and ash.
- when we cook food the colour and taste is changed so that we can eat it—the food must be cooked properly so that it is not undercooked or overcooked.
- when living things die they will start to rot or decompose and we can smell the changes that are taking place.

Chemical changes are taking place all around us and even inside us. When plants grow or animals digest food, chemical changes take place.

Chemical changes can be slow, such as an iron roof or a car body rusting. Or they can be fast, such as burning fuel in an engine or rocket. Burning is always a chemical change and is usually fast.

Many chemical changes are useful. For example, the food that you eat is changed in your body. The chemical changes make new substances to help your body grow and give you energy. Other chemical changes are not useful. For example, if you keep food too long, chemical changes take place, spoiling the food. When you chew betel nut with lime, it can lead to cancer of the mouth, which is harmful.

Some chemical changes are useful, such as the changes in your body that help you grow.

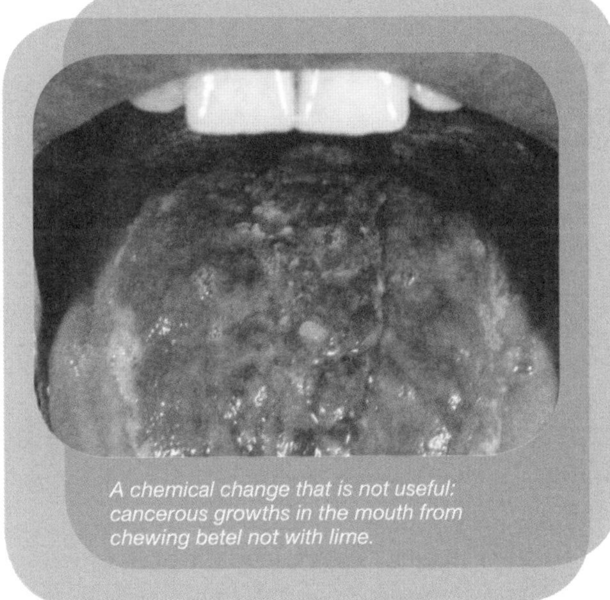

A chemical change that is not useful: cancerous growths in the mouth from chewing betel not with lime.

Chemical changes can be slow, such as iron and steel changing to rust.

Chemical changes can be fast, such as fuel burning in an outboard motor.

Chemical reactions

When chemical changes take place, we say that a chemical reaction has taken place. The original substances that are used up in chemical reaction are called **reactants**. The new substances that are formed in a chemical change are called products. The new substances usually look different from the original substances and have different properties.

Signs of a chemical change

When a chemical change takes place:

- one or more new substances are formed
- energy is given out or taken in
- the change is usually difficult to reverse.

Particles and chemical change

Elements are the simplest kind of matter and there are over 100 elements. Every substance in the world is made of elements. However, most substances are made up of two or more elements joined together. Substances that are made of two or more elements joined together are called **compounds**.

During a chemical reaction, the particles of the reactants are rearranged to form the particles of the products. No particles are lost. For example, magnesium is a metal element that is silver-grey in colour. When magnesium is held in a flame it burns with a bright, white light and gives off a lot of energy. The metal changes to a white powder. Particles of the element magnesium join with particles of the element oxygen to form a new substance called magnesium oxide. This chemical reaction can be represented by the word equation:

magnesium *plus* oxygen *equals* magnesium oxide

magnesium + oxygen → magnesium oxide

0 0 00

The number of particles of each element is the same after the chemical reaction as it was before. The particles of the reactants have been combined in a different way to form a new particle.

When magnesium burns in air it reacts with oxygen to form magnesium oxide. During this chemical change, a large amount of light and heat energy is released.

Energy and chemical change

Many chemical reactions give off light and heat. For example, magnesium is used in the flashlights of cameras. The bright flash you see when a picture is taken is the burning of a small amount of magnesium inside the flash bulb.

Magnesium is used in camera flashbulbs.

All chemical changes involve energy. However, not all chemical reactions give off energy. Some chemical changes must have energy added before a reaction can take place.

Every substance in the world contains stored energy, but some substances contain more energy than others.

- If the products formed during a chemical reaction have *less* stored energy than the reactants, then energy must have been given off.
- If the products formed during a chemical reaction have *more* stored energy than the reactants, then energy must have been taken in or supplied.

All chemical reactions result in an increase or decrease of stored energy. The energy taken in or given out may be in the form of heat, light, sound or electrical energy.

When we light a fire and cook food we are using the following energy changes:

- Wood contains a lot of stored energy. This energy originally came from the Sun when many chemical reactions took place inside the living tree.
- When the wood is burned more chemical reactions take place.
- New substances such as ash and smoke are formed and a lot of heat and light energy is given off. Some sound energy is also given off.
- During cooking, the heat energy causes chemical reactions to take place in the food and the raw substances change to new substances.

When wood burns a chemical reaction takes place and heat energy is given out. When food cooks, chemical changes take place as energy is taken in.

Heating iron and sulphur

When a mixture of iron filings and sulphur is heated, it glows red. The yellow sulphur colour disappears and is replaced by a black solid. The substance is no longer a mixture of the elements sulphur and iron and a magnet cannot be used to separate the iron filings from the solid. A chemical reaction has taken place to form a new substance.

The heat has caused the iron particles and the sulphur particles to join up to form particles of a new substance called iron sulphide. The reaction can be described using this word equation:

iron + sulphur → iron sulphide

0 **0** **00**

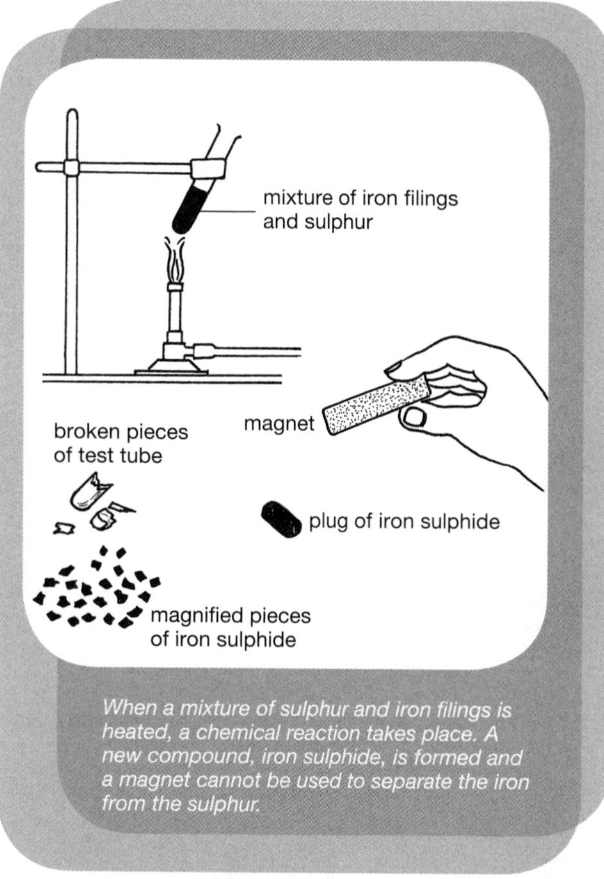

When a mixture of sulphur and iron filings is heated, a chemical reaction takes place. A new compound, iron sulphide, is formed and a magnet cannot be used to separate the iron from the sulphur.

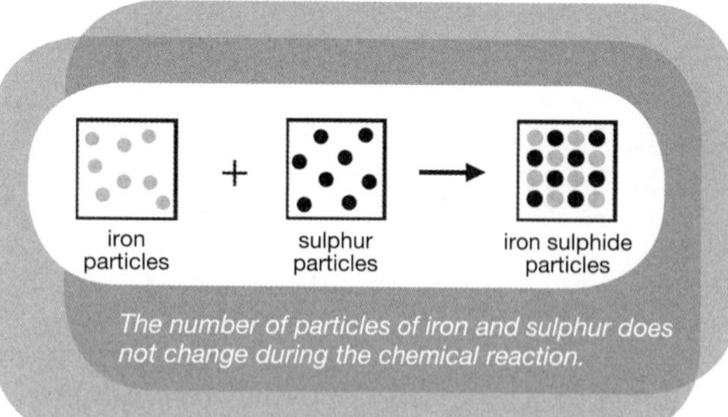

The number of particles of iron and sulphur does not change during the chemical reaction.

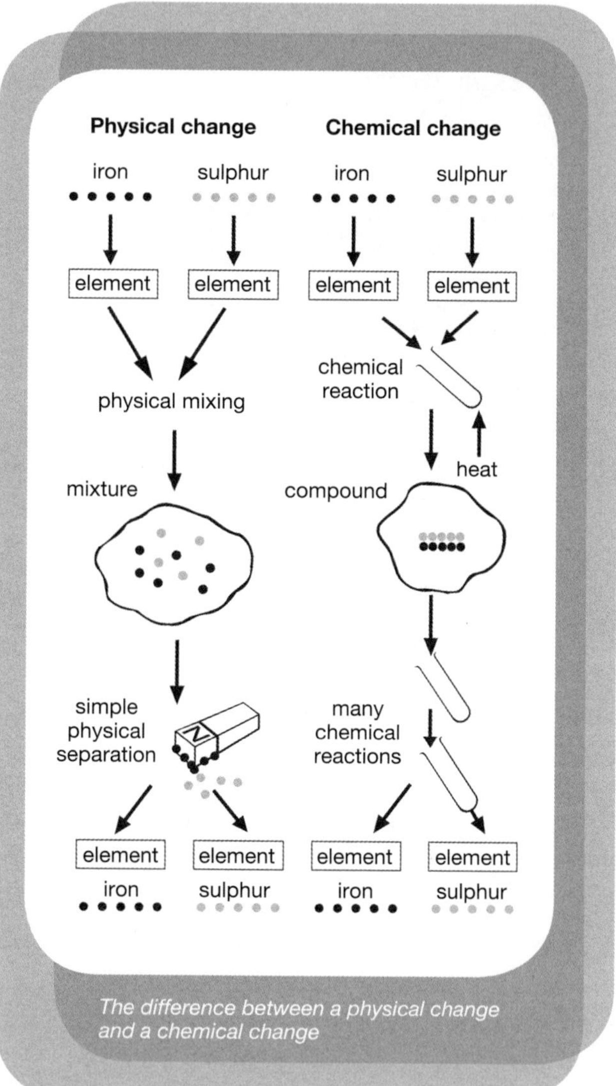

The difference between a physical change and a chemical change

For you to try

1 **Investigation: Leaving potato crisps in the air**

   a Collect a packet of potato crisps or chips, a plate and a cover such as a tea towel or piece of cloth.

   b Open one packet of crisps and taste one of them. Describe the taste and the noise made as you eat the crisp.

   c Spread the rest out on a plate or dish and cover them with a cloth. Air should be able to reach the crisps.

   d Put them in a place where they will not be reached by insects or other animals (not in a refrigerator).

   e Leave the crisps for several days, but observe them and taste one of them each day.

   f Write down your results and again describe what happens to the taste and the noise made as you eat the crisp.

   g Discuss your results and try to explain them. What changes have taken place?

   h How can you tell if a chemical change has taken place?

2 What is the difference between a physical and a chemical change?

3 Copy and complete this table to show which changes are physical and which are chemical:

	Type of change	
Example of change	**Physical**	**Chemical**
Coffee beans drying in the sun		
Candle wax melting		
Iron rusting		
Sharpening a bush knife		
A match burning		
Meat being cooked		
Putting coffee into hot water		
Grass cuttings decaying		
Peeling vegetables		
Digesting food		
Cleaning a paintbrush with water		

4 List four useful chemical changes that occur around your home.
5 List four chemical changes that are not useful. Explain why they are not useful.
6 During each of the following chemical changes there is a change in appearance. For each change, describe the appearance of the new substance and the new substance formed.
   a raw egg ➔ cooked egg
   b iron ➔ rust
   c magnesium ➔ magnesium oxide
7 In groups, design and carry out your own simple experiments to show a physical change and a chemical change. Write about your experiment using the scientific method and show your experiment to the other groups.
8 Write simple word equations to describe the following chemical changes:
   a wood burning in a fire
   b sweet potato cooking in a saucepan of water
   c meat cooking in a frying pan
   d a fishing hook going rusty
   e an old battery or dry cell that is leaking chemicals from inside.

Using heat, light and sound energy

Humans use many different types of energy. For example, in Papua New Guinea we often use electricity, **solar** energy, water and wind energy. Other types of energy include heat and light, sound, food, potential, kinetic, chemical and nuclear.

Energy that can travel through space and air in the form of electro-magnetic rays is called **radiant energy**. Some examples of radiant energy and its uses and effects are shown in the table:

Type of radiant energy	Uses and effects
Heat	Cooking, heating the house
Light	Plants use light to make food. Many animals use light to see. People use light when they take photographs.
Radio waves	Communication
Microwaves	Cooking, communication
Infra-red rays	Heating
Ultra-violet rays	The Sun gives out ultra-violet rays that burn the skin
X-rays	Looking inside the body or suitcases at airports

Heat energy

Heat energy cooks our food and warms our homes in cold places. Heat from burning fuel is used to run engines in cars, trucks, boats and aeroplanes. Heat is also used to:

- cut and weld metals
- separate metals from rocks that contain minerals
- make petrol and diesel from crude oil
- shape metals and plastic
- make glass, paper, textiles and many other products.

Sources of heat include the Sun, fuels like firewood and kerosene, electric stoves and jugs, matches and candles. Heat can also come from under the ground. The rocks deep inside the Earth are very hot and they are **molten** in some places. We know that there is still molten rock deep inside the Earth because it sometimes comes to the surface when a volcano erupts. In some places the hot rocks are found near the surface. The hot rocks cause steam, hot gases, boiling water and mud which are found in many parts of Papua New Guinea. Examples are Lihir Island in New Ireland, Lou Island in Manus and Kairiru Island in the East Sepik.

At Salamo in Milne Bay the hot springs are used for bathing, washing clothes and even cooking. In East and West New Britain and Bougainville, the megapode bird lays its eggs in mounds of sand that are kept warm by heat from hot rocks. The warm sand helps to incubate the eggs and make them hatch. People help to look after the mounds and the birds because they are an important source of food.

In some parts of the world this heat is used to turn water into steam. The steam is used to make electricity and is called **geothermal** energy. Electricity is made from geothermal energy in New Zealand, Italy and Iceland.

A megapode bird

Light energy

Light is a form of energy. Sunlight is the most important example because it is needed to make plants grow. Light also allows us to see and helps us to take photographs and make films.

When we heat things they often give off light. A wood fire gives off light, so do torches made from dried coconut fronds, kerosene lamps and candles. Torches give light that comes from the globe or bulb and electrical energy from the battery. Cars and trucks also have bulbs in the headlights. Buildings that have electricity usually have lights that use bulbs or fluorescent tubes. Towns and cities have street lights and some sports ovals have floodlights to allow people to play sport at night when it is cooler. At Koki in Port Moresby, street lights have been placed around the courts to allow people to play basketball at night.

Car lights at night

Sound energy

Sound is a form of energy. When you hear something you are detecting the sound. Sounds are made whenever something vibrates. When you talk, vocal cords inside your throat vibrate rapidly. The vibrating cords cause particles of air to vibrate. The vibrations in the air reach a thin piece of skin inside the ear called the **ear drum**. The vibrating ear drum causes tiny parts inside your ear to move and produce special signals which travel along nerves to the brain. Your brain then interprets the signals as sounds.

Musical instruments produce sounds because something inside the instrument vibrates. A kundu drum has a stretched skin that vibrates when you hit it. A guitar or ukulele has strings that vibrate when they are played. The hollow bamboo tubes used in a bamboo band contain air. The air vibrates when we hit the end of the tube with a rubber thong.

Science in the village: Musical instruments

In Papua New Guinea people use their **traditional knowledge** to make many different kinds of instruments using materials that they find in the local environment. All of these instruments use vibrations to make sound energy.

The *kundu* drum is the most common musical instrument in Papua New Guinea, which is widely used for traditional singing and dancing. The kundu is also part of the National Emblem which represents the country. One of the ends is covered with the stretched skin of a lizard, which also has beads resin to help tune the drum. When we hit the skin with our hand the skin vibrates which makes the air inside vibrate and the sound comes out of the open end.

The slit drum or *garamut* is made from a log that is hollowed out. When the drum is hit with a stick it makes the air inside vibrate and the hollow shape acts as a sound box to make the sound bigger. Garamuts can be used to send messages to people who are a long way away.

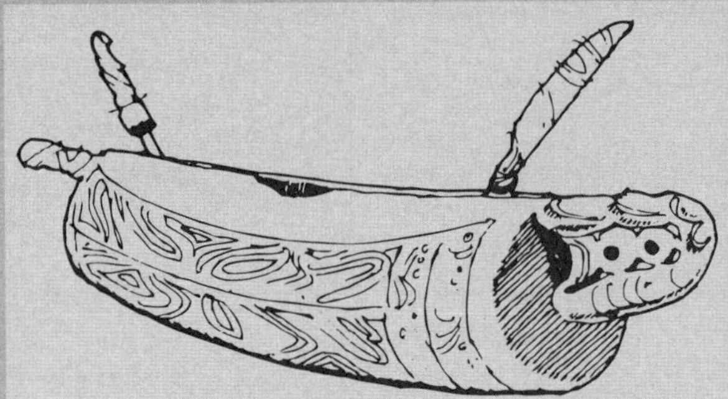

The *Jew's harp* or *jaw harp* is made from a piece of bamboo that is cut so that one strip is free to vibrate inside a frame. The player makes the strip vibrate with a finger while holding the bamboo frame against the lips or teeth. Changing the shape of the mouth and the amount of air inside it changes the sound that is made.

Flutes and *whistles* may be made from a single piece of bamboo or a conch shell. A hole is made in the bamboo or conch shell and the player must blow across the hole. Pan-pipe flutes are made by tying different lengths of bamboo together and blowing over the top of them.

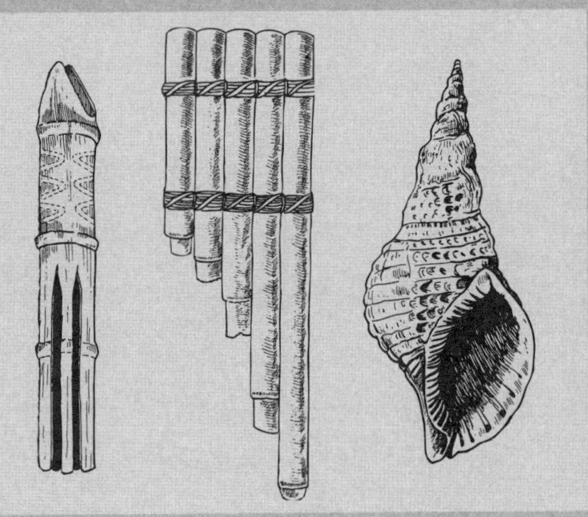

For you to try

1 **Investigation: Feel the vibrations**

- **a** Collect a radio and a balloon.
- **b** Blow up the balloon and tie the end.
- **c** Turn on the radio.
- **d** Hold the balloon about 10 cm away from the radio. What do you feel?
- **e** Turn up the volume of the radio and hold the balloon again. What do you feel now?
- **f** Write up a scientific report to explain what you did and what you found out.

2 **Investigation: Watch sound travel**

- **a** Collect an old plastic bottle, a plastic bag, an elastic band, a candle and a pair of scissors.
- **b** Cut the bottom off the bottle.
- **c** Cut a piece of plastic to cover the end of the bottle.
- **d** Stretch the piece of plastic over the end of the bottle and hold it with an elastic band.
- **e** Light the candle and hold the bottle 2 or 3 cm away from the flame.
- **f** Tap the piece of plastic sharply with your fingertips. What happens?
- **g** Write a scientific report to say what you did and what you found out.

3 **Investigation: Changing sound**

- **a** Collect short pieces of bamboo or plastic tube or straws, a strip of flat timber or stiff card, rubber band or strips of rubber inner tube.
- **b** Tie tubes or straws of different lengths to the strip of wood or stiff cardboard using the rubber band.
- **c** Blow across the ends of the tubes.
- **d** Describe what happens.

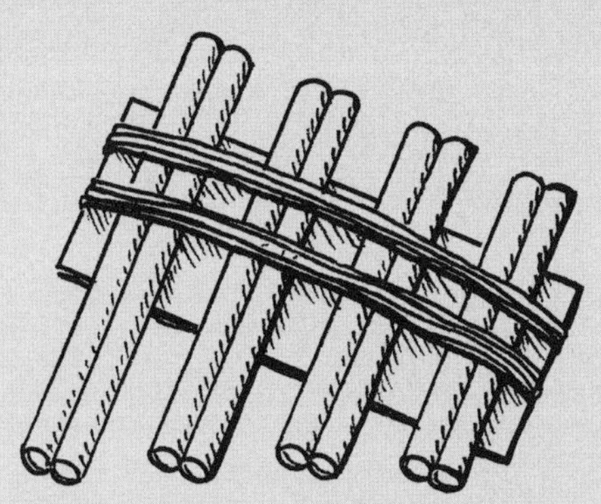

4 **Investigation: Bottle sounds**

- **a** Collect two identical glass bottles, some water and a spoon.
- **b** Fill the bottles with different amounts of water.

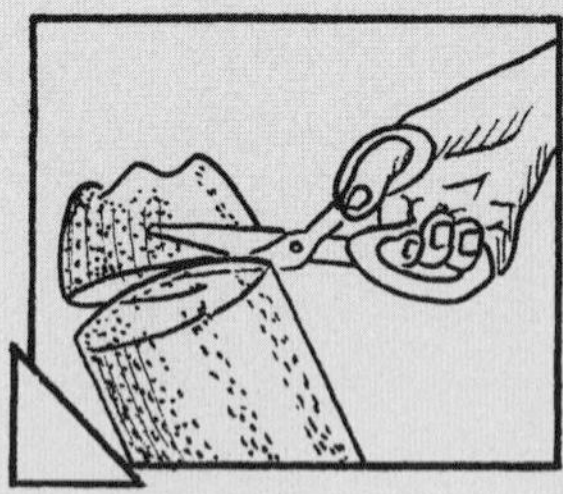

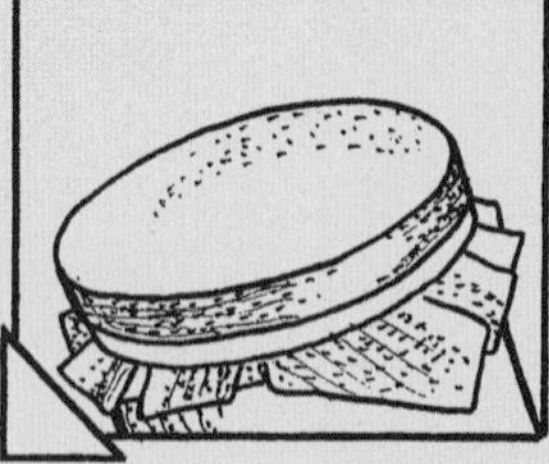

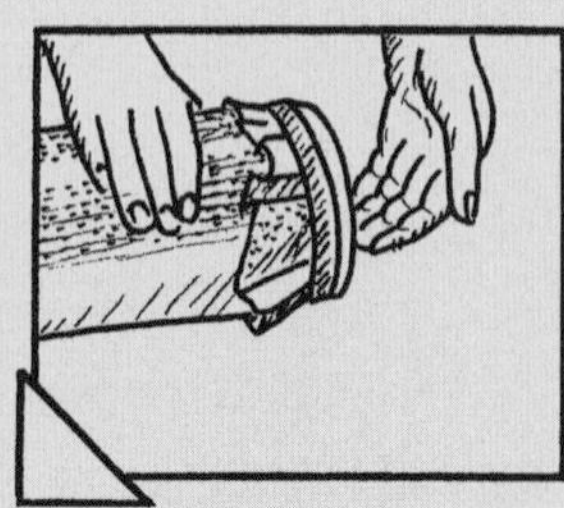

c Blow across the top of each of the bottles. Which one makes the higher note?

d Tap each of the bottles with a spoon. Which one makes the higher note?

e Draw a diagram of the two bottles to show the different sounds that are made from blowing and tapping with a spoon. Show the different results on the same diagram.

5 Copy and complete the following table to show the instruments that are used in your area, how the sound is made and which part vibrates.

Name of instrument	How is the sound made?	Which part vibrates?

6 Describe some examples of the way that heat, light and sound energy are used to help people in your community. In each case describe the energy change that takes place, how the energy is used or the effect. Also give one example of the way in which heat, light or sound is not helpful or might be harmful.

7 Make a poster to show the different ways that people use heat in different places such as at home, in the garden, in the store, at work or when travelling.

Other types of energy

Food energy

Food is one of our most important needs. Food provides us with energy for walking, running, working, playing sport, thinking and breathing. Food is also used to build and repair our bodies. Without food we cannot live long.

The kind of food people eat, and the amount they eat, varies from province to province and from country to country. There is also a big difference in the way people prepare, serve and eat food. This is mainly due to differences in climate and culture.

Energy is measured in units called **kilojoules** (symbol kJ). One kilojoule equals one thousand joules. Different foods have different amounts of energy. For example, foods that contain a lot of fat also have a lot of energy.

The amount of energy required by the human body depends on such things as body size and weight, age, sex, physical activity and climate. Generally, lighter people need less energy from food than heavier people, and females require less energy than males. When we eat food that contains more energy than we need we become overweight.

For you to try

1 Explain why you need food. When might you require more food than normal?

Potential energy

Potential energy is often called stored energy. Energy can be stored in a number of ways. For example:

- compressing a spring
- holding water in a dam or tank
- stretching a piece of **elastic**.

A coconut hanging from a tree and water sitting in a tank on top of a roof both have gravitational potential energy. Anything that is able to fall because of the force of **gravity** has gravitational potential energy.

Springs and stretched or wound up rubber bands have elastic potential energy. An object has elastic potential energy if it is able to return to its original shape or position. The springs on a car and the rubber of a slingshot or spear gun have elastic potential energy.

Examples of things that have potential energy

Kinetic energy

Kinetic energy is the energy of movement. When something moves we say that it has kinetic energy. A truck moving along the road, a canoe being carried down a river, a person jumping over a drain on the side of the road all have energy. The faster something moves the more kinetic energy it has. This is why it hurts more to be hit by a fast ball than a slow ball when you are playing sport. Kinetic energy also increases with the mass of the object. A speeding truck or car has a lot more kinetic energy than a fast-moving ball. An object that is not moving has no kinetic energy.

Forces in everyday life

Starting and stopping

We use forces every day to lift, push and pull things. A force is always needed to make something move. Whenever we are pushing or pulling, stretching or squashing, bending, twisting or tearing we are exerting a force.

Scientists say that a force can be a push or a pull. For example, when we want to move a heavy rock or stone we can push it to make it roll. When we want a bucket of water from a well we can pull it up using a rope.

It is sometimes difficult to start things moving, especially if they are heavy. Once something heavy is moving it is difficult to make it stop. Things stay still or keep moving because of something called **inertia**. A big rock has so much inertia that you cannot make it move by pushing against it with a big force.

Wearing seatbelts is a good example of reducing the effect of inertia. When a car crashes it is forced to stop suddenly, but the passengers must be made to stop too. If the passengers are not wearing seatbelts they will keep moving forwards because of their inertia and they could be thrown through the windscreen.

Wearing seatbelts saves lives in car accidents.

For you to try

1 **Investigation: Fruit drop**

a Collect a mug, a matchbox cover, a piece of card and a lemon or similar fruit.

b Lay the card on the mug.

c Stand the matchbox cover on the card and balance the lemon on top of it.

d Pull the card out quickly and observe what happens.

e Explain your observations.

2 **Investigation: Five coin trick**

a Collect five identical coins like 20t, 50t or K1 and a table knife.

b Put the coins in a pile and knock the bottom coin with the back edge of a table knife.

c Observe what happens and explain your observations.

Speeding up and slowing down

Forces can make things speed up. For example, you can walk or cycle faster by exerting a greater force with your legs. The driver of a truck can go faster by pushing down on the accelerator. This gives more fuel to the engine which provides a bigger force.

There are also forces that make things slow down or stop, like the force of the brakes on a bicycle or holding a paddle flat against the water to make a canoe slow down. A parachute can also be used to slow something when it is falling.

When a truck moves along a straight road at a steady speed the forces acting on it are balanced. There is the force of the engine driving it forwards and the force of **friction** trying to slow it down.

A PMV bus speeding down a hill

When the driver puts the brakes on, the truck slows down. This is because the force of friction and the force applied by the brakes are greater than the force from the engine. In this case the forces are unbalanced. Unbalanced forces make things go faster or slower.

When something is not moving then the forces are also balanced. For example, when you stand on the branch of a tree your weight acts downwards and there is another force, called the reaction force, which acts upwards. You do not fall because the two forces are balanced. They are equal but act in the opposite direction. Most people do not think about this but if the branch breaks your weight will be greater than the reaction force and you will fall and speed up until you hit the ground.

Forces can act in any direction. When something is already moving a force can be used to make it change direction. For example, if a ball is moving in one direction you can hit it to make it change direction.

Things which are moving always travel in a straight line unless something forces them to change direction. When you are travelling in a truck and you go quickly round a corner you will feel yourself being pushed against the side of the truck.

For you to try

1 Investigation: Turn the corner

a Collect the lid from a cardboard carton and a small coin.

b Put the coin in the middle of the lid. Push the lid forwards and then turn it sharply to one side.

c Observe what happens to the coin.

d Explain your observations.

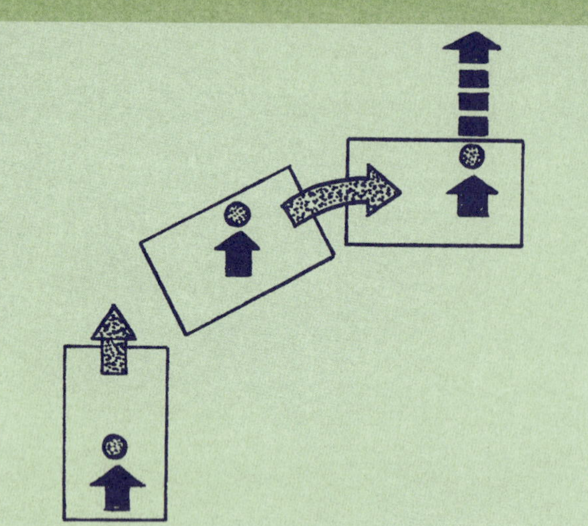

2 Investigation : Swing the bucket

a Collect a bucket and half fill it with water.

b Stand outside, away from other people, and swing it around in a circle.

c Observe what happens to the water in the bucket.

d Explain your observations.

3 **Investigation: Lift the ball**

a Collect a glass jar and a ball of plasticine about the size of a marble.

b Put the ball of plasticine on a table and put the mouth of the jar over the ball.

c Turn the jar in a circle so that the ball starts spinning inside the jar.

d Lift the jar from the table and observe what happens to the ball.

e Explain your observations.

Types of forces

There are four main types of forces.

1 The force of gravity

The force of gravity is the attraction of one object for another. When we jump up, the force of gravity pulls us back down again towards the centre of the Earth. For this reason, the direction of 'down' varies from one part of the world to another. For a person in Papua New Guinea the direction of down is opposite from the direction of down for a person in Guinea in West Africa because these two places are on opposite sides of the world.

The force of gravity pulling on an object is also called **weight**. Weight is the pull of gravity that

- holds things on the surface of the Earth
- makes things fall back to the ground when they are thrown in the air
- holds **planets** and **satellites** in orbit.

The sea is also affected by the pull of the gravity of the Moon, which causes high and low **tides**.

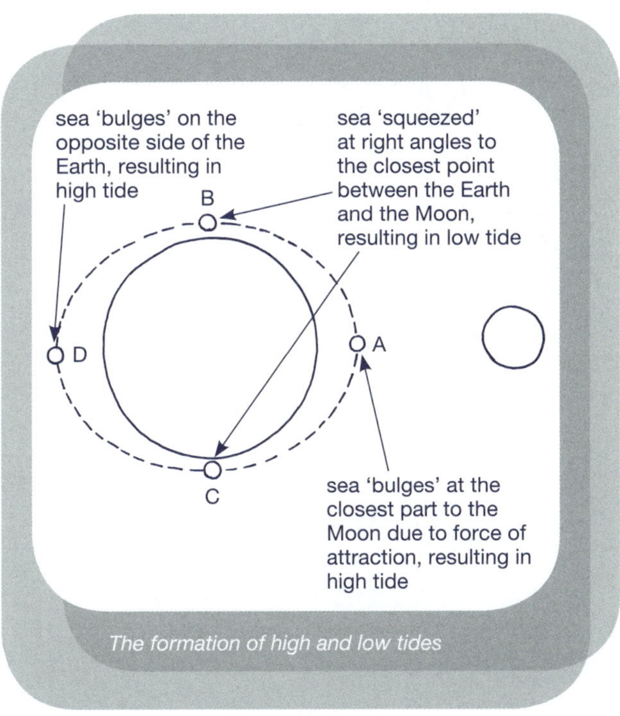

The formation of high and low tides

The force of gravity also pulls the particles of air in the **atmosphere** towards the Earth. The way that the air presses down on the Earth is called **atmospheric pressure**. You cannot feel air pushing in on you because your body pushes outwards with the same force as the air. As you move further away from the Earth there are fewer particles of air and there is less pressure. We say that the air is 'thinner' and this is why people have difficulty breathing on high mountains like Mt Wilhelm, and may get mountain sickness.

In outer space there is no air and so astronauts have to wear special space suits that push against their bodies with the same force as the air on Earth.

Astronauts wear special space suits because there is no air in space.

The force of gravity also affects the growth of plants. For example, roots respond to the force of gravity by growing downwards, while the shoot grows upwards. Roots can find water and minerals in the soil by growing downwards and the shoot grows upwards towards the light needed for photosynthesis.

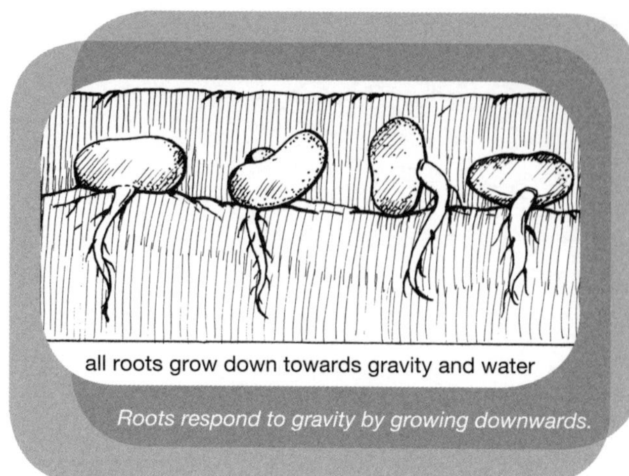

Roots respond to gravity by growing downwards.

2 Magnetic forces

Magnetic forces are caused by magnets. Magnets are usually made of iron and attract things that are made of iron or steel. Magnets are often found inside the plastic strip on the door of a refrigerator or freezer and used to make the door close. Magnets are also used in compasses, electric motors and generators, radios and computers.

3 Electrical forces

Electrical forces are caused by charged objects. For example, clothes that are made from synthetic material will try to stick to our bodies. Sometimes the material makes a little crackling noise when we take it off and we might also feel the hairs on our body stand up because of the charge.

4 Elastic forces

Elastic forces can make objects change shape. A foam rubber mattress, a spring, a rubber ball and a pair of thongs are examples in which elastic forces can act.

The way that forces act

Some forces act on objects from a distance. The force does not have to be touching the object in order to make the object change. Other forces need to be in contact with the object before these forces can change the way the object is moving or altering its shape.

The table below shows some forces that act at a distance and others that act when they make contact.

Different ways that forces act	
Forces that act over a distance	**Forces that act on contact**
The force of gravity	Explosive forces e.g. a bomb exploding
Magnetic forces	Friction
Electrical forces	Collision forces e.g. a car crash

For you to try

1 Make a list of the forces that act around you during the day and night.

2 Design an investigation to find out how forces can be used to slow down a moving object. For example:

- **a** Tie a stone inside a small piece of cloth.
- **b** Make a parachute from a square of material.
- **c** Tie the parachute to the stone in the cloth using four strings, one to each corner of the parachute.
- **d** Neatly wrap the stone inside the parachute so that it can easily unfold and throw it in the air a number of times (or drop if from a high place).
- **e** Observe what happens and, if possible, measure the time taken for the parachute to fall. Record your result.
- **f** Repeat the investigation with different types of parachutes and again record your result.
- **g** Try different sizes and shapes of parachute, different kinds of material, different lengths of string, try putting holes in the parachute etc.
- **h** Which ones work best?

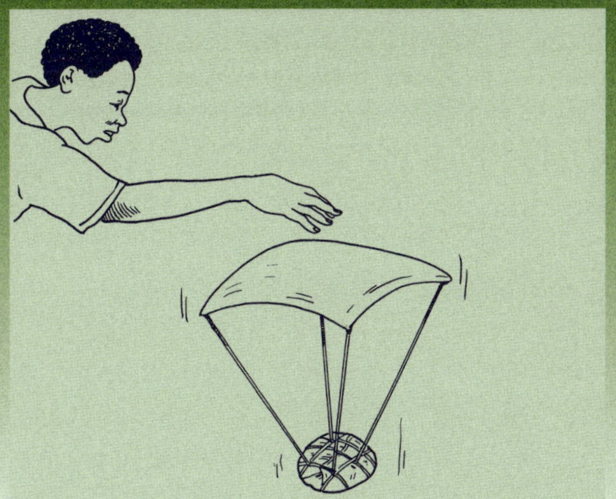

3 Make a list of forces that slow things down.

4 Make a list of forces that speed things up.

5 **Investigation: How air pushes**

- **a** Collect a bowl or bucket of water, a drinking glass or jam jar and a piece of paper.
- **b** Crumple a piece of paper and push it into the bottom of a glass so that it cannot fall out.
- **c** Push the glass straight down into a bowl of water.
- **d** What happens to the paper?
- **e** Where is the water level inside the glass?

f Describe what you did and explain what you have found out.

6 Investigation: The force of air

a Collect a large plastic shopping bag and a big book. The bag must not have any holes.

b Lay the plastic shopping bag flat on the table so that the open end hangs over the edge.

c Put the big book on the bag.

d Gather the open end of the bag and make a mouthpiece and blow steadily into the bag. Observe what happens.

e Put a heavy weight such a rock on the book or ask another student to sit on the book and repeat the experiment. Observe what happens.

f Write a scientific report of your investigation to explain what you did and what you found out.

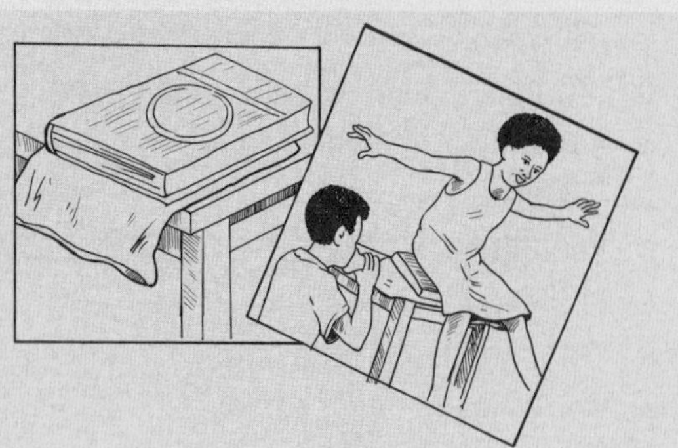

7 Investigation: Tug-of-war

a Collect a piece of rope, bush vine or several laplaps tied together

b Make two equal groups of students. Use the rope or laplaps tied together to have a tug-of-war.

c Repeat with different students in each team or group.

d Draw a diagram to explain what happens. Use arrows to show the direction and size of the forces.

e Try mixing different combinations of big people and small people, boys and girls on each side. What happens?

f Write a scientific report of your investigation describing balanced and unbalanced forces.

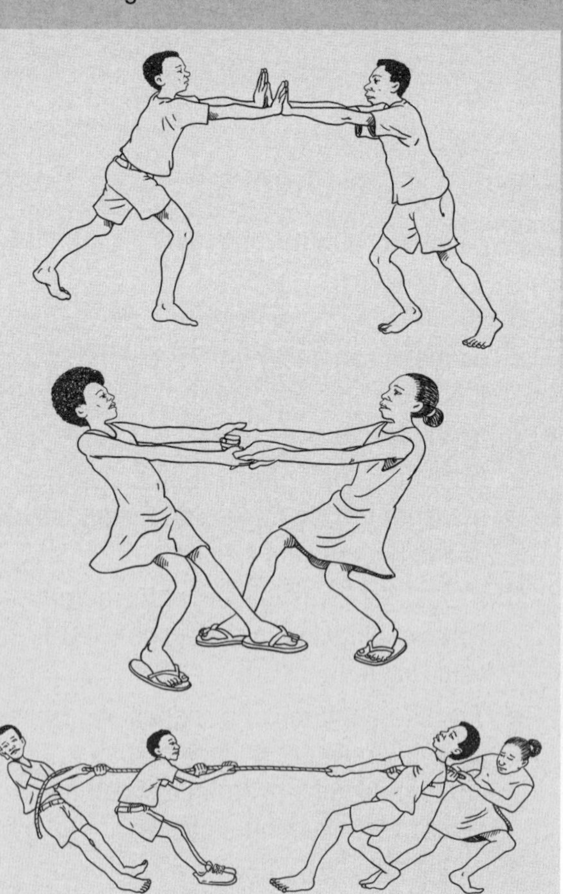

8 Investigation: Four against one

- **a** Collect two strong, smooth sticks or broom handles, a long rope and some talcum powder.
- **b** Work in groups of five students.
- **c** Tie one end of the rope to one of the sticks and then loop it from one stick to the other in a zigzag pattern.
- **d** Two people hold each stick and try to pull them apart while you pull on the end of the rope. It works better if you put a little talcum powder on the sticks so that the rope can slide easily
- **e** What happens? Can one person pull against four others?
- **f** Swap over so that everyone gets a turn on the end of the rope. Do you always get the same result?
- **g** Write a scientific report of your investigation describing balanced and unbalanced forces.

Understanding friction

Friction is the force that slows things down or makes them stop moving. Friction occurs whenever one object slides over another. For example, there is friction between your hands when you rub them together. There is also friction between your feet and the ground when you walk.

The force used to drive a truck along a level road is used to overcome the friction that tries to slow it down, such as:

- the drag of the air on the truck
- the friction between the moving parts of the truck
- the friction between the tyres and the road.

The force of friction occurs because objects are never completely smooth even though they may look smooth. The roughness of the two surfaces in contact means there are many points that do not slide easily over each other.

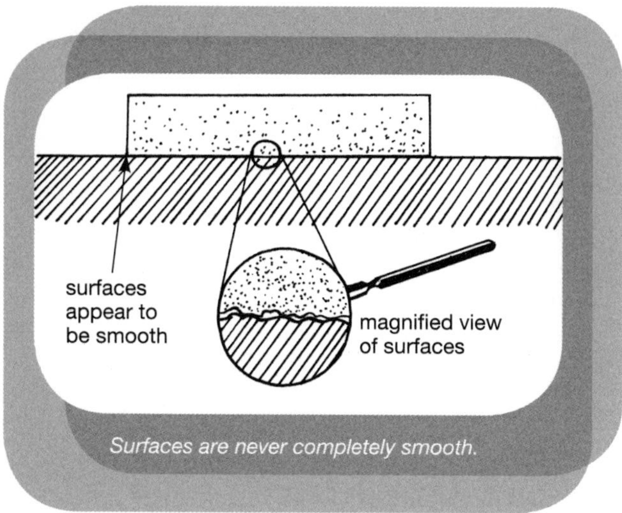

Surfaces are never completely smooth.

The size of the force of friction depends upon the following:

1 The *roughness* of the two surfaces that are rubbing against each other. Rough surfaces have a bigger area of contact that helps the grip and stops slipping. Smooth surfaces have less points of contact and slide more easily. As a result, rough surfaces have more friction than smooth surfaces. This is why car tyres and sports shoes have a rough tread and must be replaced when they wear out and lose their grip. The tiny ridges on the tips of your fingers that make your fingerprint also help you to grip things and so do the jaws of a pair of pliers.

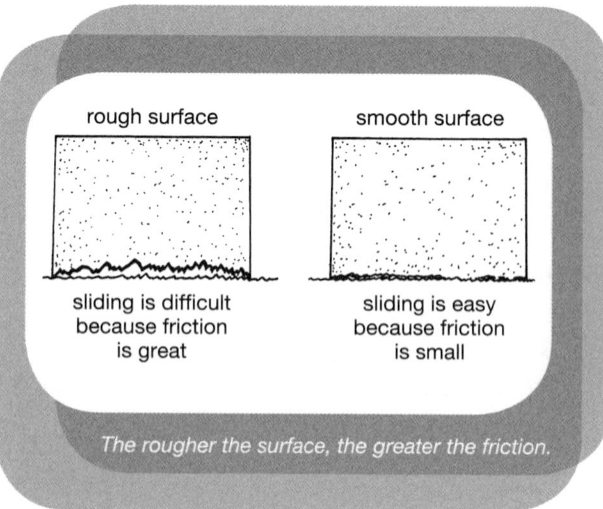

The rougher the surface, the greater the friction.

2 The *force pushing* the two surfaces together. It is much easier to slide an empty box over the floor because the force between the box and the floor is much less than a box that has something heavy inside.

Friction can be a problem because it makes things wear out and makes things hot. When you rub your hands together you can feel the heat produced by friction. The moving parts of a machine can also get hot which can make them expand too much and stop working. But when we strike a match we need the heat from the friction to make the match catch alight.

So friction has advantages and disadvantages. The main advantage of friction is that it allows things to move. For example, when we ride a bicycle friction is needed between your feet and the pedals and between the tyre and the road to make the bicycle move. Friction is needed between the rubber brake blocks and the rim of the wheel to make the bicycle stop. However, friction in the chain and wheel **bearings** slows you down, which is a disadvantage. Wind resistance also slows you down.

Reducing friction

Reducing the friction between the moving parts of a machine means that less energy is needed to make the machine work. Also, there is less wear of the moving parts and they do not get as hot.

Friction can be reduced in a number of different ways.

Lubrication

Machines run smoothly when their moving surfaces are covered in a thin layer of oil. Adding oil or grease so that the surfaces of moving parts slide over each other more easily is called **lubrication**. Oil and grease are called **lubricants**. This is important in engines, gearboxes, and other machines. Car and truck engines have a **dipstick** to check the level of the oil. The oil and the oil filter need to be changed or replaced regularly because they get dirty.

Bearings

Ball bearings and roller bearings are used in bicycles, cars and other types of machines. Bearings make the surfaces roll over one another rather than slide over one another and are usually lubricated with grease. Bearings reduce the friction by a large amount.

Smoothing

Surfaces that are in contact can be made smooth so that they slide over one another more easily. Traditionally, a coarse abrasive stone and the leaves of some of the 'sandpaper' figs are used to make wood smooth. For example, canoes are made as smooth as possible on the outside so that they can slide through the water without being slowed down too much. The moving parts in an engine are also made to be very smooth to reduce friction.

Oiling a bicycle makes it run smoothly.

Smoothing the outside of a canoe reduces the friction with water.

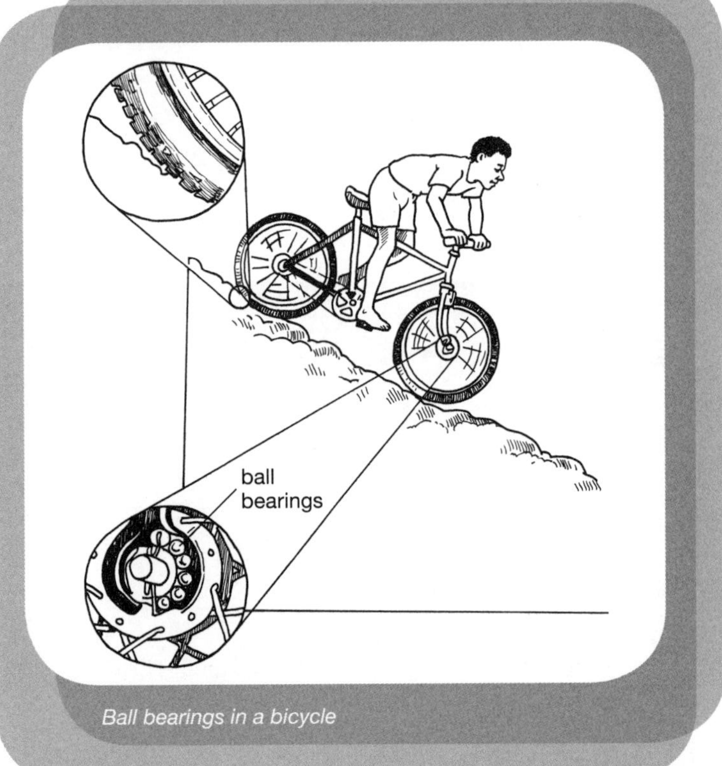

Ball bearings in a bicycle

Streamlining

Aeroplanes, rockets, racing boats and racing motor cycles are all shaped in a special way. They are **streamlined** to reduce friction with the air or water. When they are moving very quickly through the air or water there is very little drag on them.

Many animals are also streamlined. Fast swimming fish and fast flying birds have streamlined shapes.

Streamlining reduces friction.

Air cushions

If air is blown between two surfaces, friction becomes very small. This is the way in which a hovercraft works.

A hovercraft has a cushion of air between it and the ground water.

For you to try

1 **Investigation: Adding oil**

a Collect a smooth, flat surface like a glass louvre blade, a piece of flat iron or smooth flat timber, a bottle top, and some cooking oil or lubricating oil.

b Flick the bottle top with your finger and thumb so it skims across the surface. How soon does friction make it stop?

c Cover the surface with a thin film of oil and skim the bottle top again. How far does it travel now?

d Explain your results.

2 **Investigation: Spinning around**

a Collect a drink can, fifteen marbles, some thin cardboard and sticky tape.

b Tape a narrow cardboard strip around the top of the can to make a collar. The collar should be deep enough to hold the marbles, with their tops just showing (see diagram).

c Stand the can on the collar without the marbles and try to spin the can. Describe what happens.

d Carefully feed the marbles underneath it. Spin the can again and describe what happens.

e Explain your results.

Increasing friction

Friction can be useful so sometimes we need to make it increase. Friction can be increased in the following ways:

1 making the surfaces rough (for example, the tread on a tyre, the teeth of a file or the side of a matchbox).

2 using a large force to hold the two surfaces together (for example, tying a knot tightly so that it does not slip, or placing a load in the back of a utility so that the back wheels do not slip so easily).

When friction is used to wear a surface away, a rough surface such as a file or sandpaper can be used.

Sometimes friction is used to generate heat. For example, when we strike a match the spark produced lights the match.

The air scoop on the back of a racing car forces the car down on to the track.

Friction can also be made larger to give a better grip. The air scoop on the back of a racing car forces the car onto the track. As a result, friction is increased between the tyres and the road and the car can go round corners more quickly.

For you to try

1 **Investigation: Rice grain friction**

a Collect a small plastic bottle, uncooked rice and a knife.

b Fill the plastic bottle with grains of rice.

c Slide the knife into the bottle full of rice until the blade and half the handle are buried in rice.

d Gently tap the bottle on the table or hit the bottle on the side to make the rice settle and then add more rice. Continue to do this until the rice is very tightly packed and you cannot squash in any more rice. Moving the knife a little will also help the rice to settle.

e Lift the knife slowly and describe what happens.

f Write up a scientific report to say what you did and what you found out.

2 **Investigation: Putting on the brakes**

a Collect a matchbox, a matchstick, a needle and some thread.

b Cut a matchstick to fit exactly across a matchbox tray.

c Use a needle to pass a thread through the ends of the tray and over the matchstick.

d Replace the matchbox lid. You can decorate the lid if you like to make it look like a spider.

e Hold the thread tight and then let it go loose.

f Explain what happens.

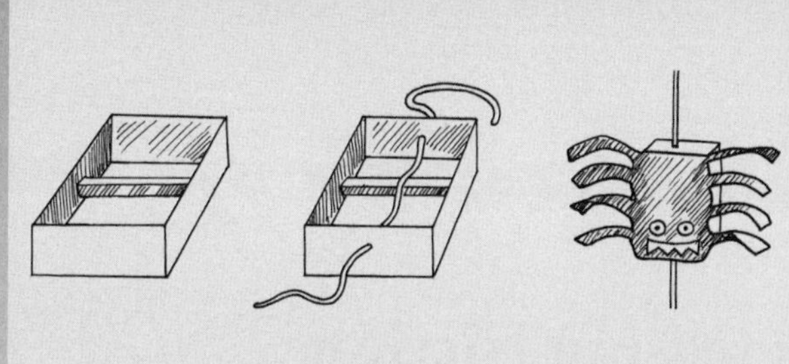

3 Draw a diagram or make a poster to show why friction acts between moving surfaces.

4 For a cyclist riding a bicycle, list:

a the places where friction needs to be large

b the places where friction needs to be small.

5 List three examples of oil being used to reduce friction.

6 Explain what would happen if the engine of a car ran out of oil.

7 For each of the following, describe how friction is reduced:

a the wheel and axle of a wheelbarrow

b a greasy pole

c a jet aeroplane flying at high speed

d the hull of a canoe

e a boat resting on logs as it is pulled out of the water.

8 The diagrams below show situations in which the force of friction acts. Copy and complete the table below to name the surfaces between which the friction is acting and describe what the force of friction is doing. The first one has been done for you.

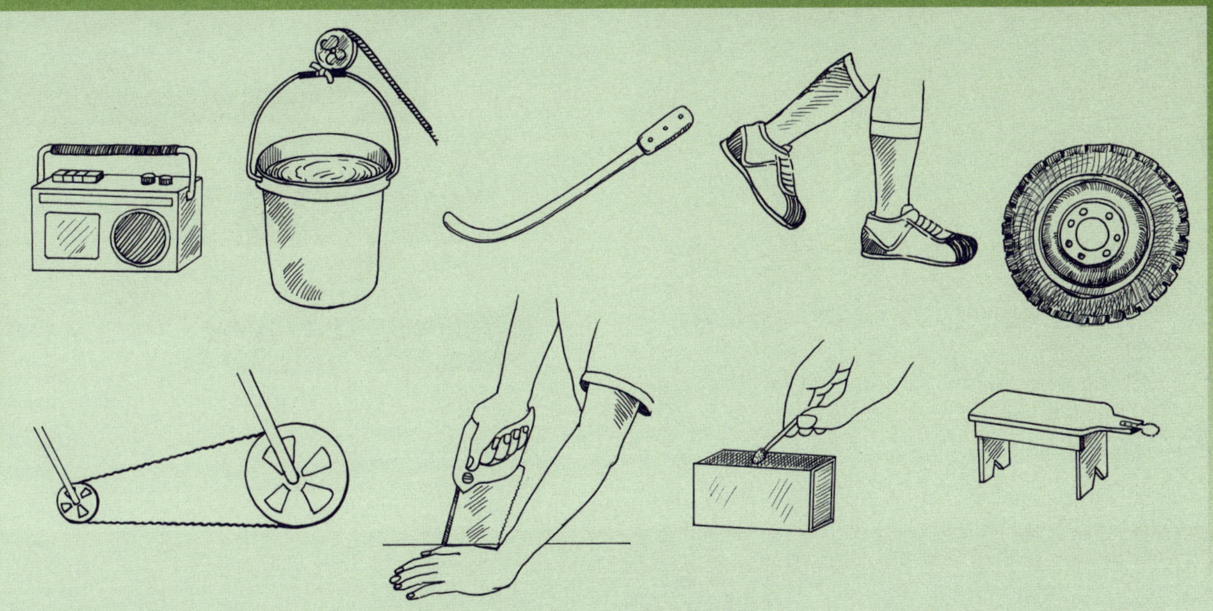

Diagram	Surfaces that the friction acts between	Friction used for
a	The person's fingers and the controls of the radio	Turning the radio on and off, tuning the radio, adjusting the volume
b		

9 Write a report on the advantages and disadvantages of friction.

Simple machines in the community

A simple machine is something that helps to make work easier. For example, it is easier to move bags of rice and cartons of fish if you put them in a wheel barrow than if you try to carry them in your arms. We say that the wheelbarrow is a simple machine.

The main types of simple machines are:

- levers
- the wheel and axle
- inclined planes
- pulleys and gear wheels.

Simple machines can do three things to help us:

1 move a heavy load with a small force
2 make things go faster
3 change the direction of a force.

The spade is a lever.

This tractor steering wheel consists of a wheel and an axle.

For you to try

1 Why are simple machines like scissors and pliers called double levers?

2 The propeller of a boat is often called a screw. Draw one and explain what it does.

3 Look at the diagram of a type of car jack called a scissor jack. What happens to the car as you turn the handle?

4 Look at the diagram of the vice that is used in a workshop to hold things that are being made or repaired. It is made of two simple machines, the screw and the wheel and axle. How does each one work so that the moveable jaw comes closer to the fixed jaw and holds the work?

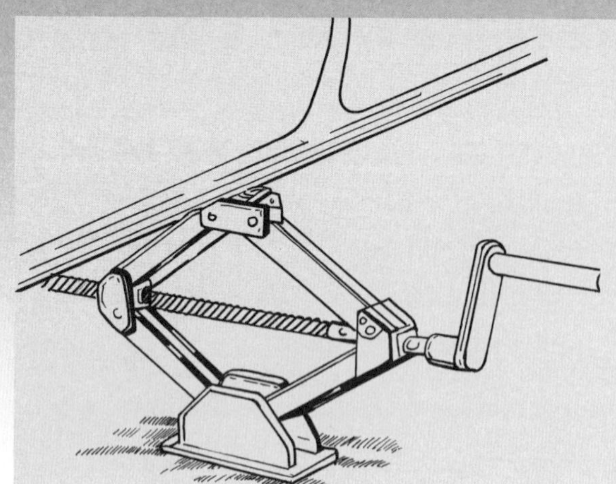

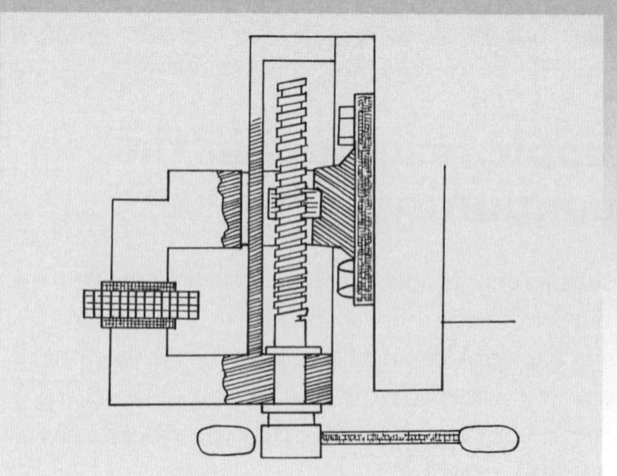

More pulleys and gear wheels

Many modern car engines have a timing belt that is made of special strong rubber that bends easily but does not stretch. Rather than being smooth and V-shaped like a fan belt, the belt is flat and has special ridges across the inside of the belt. The pulleys are not smooth but have grooves for the ridges on the belt to fit into. The timing belt is used to open the valves that allow fuel to enter the engine and exhaust gases to leave the engine. This special kind of belt has some of the advantages of a belt and some of the advantages of a chain and **gears**. The timing belt in an engine is very important. If the timing belt stretches or breaks the engine will not work and could also be badly damaged.

A car engine

For you to try

1. Look at the engine of a truck or car and identify the bottom pulley, fan belt, and the pulleys of the fan, alternator and water pump. The engine should not be running. It is dangerous to put your fingers near a running engine. Draw a diagram to show how the pulleys and belt move. What will happen to the engine if the fan belt breaks or comes off the pulley?
2. Two students are riding their bicycles side by side. One is pedalling faster than the other, even though they are travelling at the same speed. Explain this.
3. What are the two most important properties of the rubber timing belt of a car or truck engine? Explain your answer.

Hydraulic machines

Hydraulic machines use a special kind of liquid called hydraulic oil to move a force from one place to another. A liquid cannot be compressed and if a force is applied to a liquid in a pipe then the force will move along the pipe to the other end. The brakes on cars and trucks work in this way. When you put your foot on the brake pedal, the force moves along the brake pipe and pushes the brake pads against the disc, which slows down the car. When you take your foot off the brake, the brake pads come away from the discs and the hydraulic oil moves back along the pipe.

The three-point linkage at the back of a tractor uses hydraulics. Excavators for digging holes in the ground, fork-lift trucks and aeroplanes all use hydraulics. Most trucks carry a hydraulic jack which also works in this way.

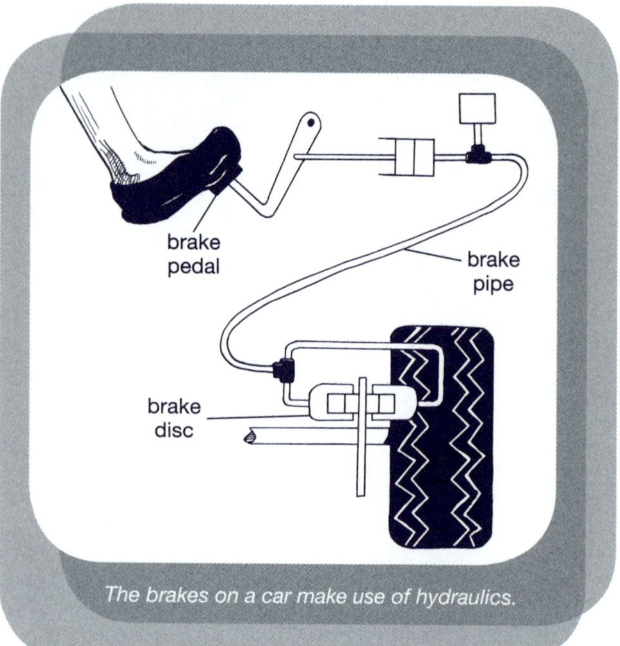

The brakes on a car make use of hydraulics.

Projects

1. Make instruments with bottles filled with different amounts of water, bamboo tubes etc., and play some tunes. Have a concert.
2. Work as a whole group with your teacher to design a short questionnaire to find out about the need for simple machines to do work in the community. Think about inside the home and outside. What work needs to be done? What simple machines can be used to help do this work?

   Analyse the findings from your questionnaire and make some recommendations. If possible, help the community to carry out one of your recommendations.

Summary questions

1 Which of the following best describes the particles in the three states of matter?

	Solid	Liquid	Gas
A	Strongly held together and cannot move past each other	Strongly held together but can move past each other	Not strongly held together so can move past each other
B	Not strongly held together so can move past each other	Strongly held together and cannot move past each other	Not strongly held together but cannot move past each other
C	Strongly held together but can move past each other	Not strongly held together and cannot move past each other	Strongly held together but can move past each other
D	Not strongly held together and cannot move past each other	Not strongly held together so can move past each other	Strongly held together and cannot move past each other

2 Which of the following best describes the size and shape of the three states of matter?

	Solid	Liquid	Gas
A	Fixed size but no fixed shape	Fixed size but no fixed shape	No fixed size or shape
B	No fixed size or shape	Fixed size and shape	Fixed size but no fixed shape
C	Fixed size and shape	No fixed size or shape	Fixed size but no fixed shape
D	Fixed size and shape	Fixed size but no fixed shape	No fixed size or shape

3 Which of the following are examples of physical changes?

I changes of state

II dissolving

III making and separating mixtures

A I and II only

B II and III only

C I and III only

D I, II and III

4 Which of the following best describes different changes of state?

	Solid to liquid	Gas to liquid	Liquid to gas	Liquid to solid
A	Melting	Condensation	Evaporation	Solidification
B	Casting	Condensation	Evaporation	Freezing
C	Dissolving	Evaporation	Condensation	Solidification
D	Solidification	Condensation	Evaporation	Freezing

5 Which of the following best describes the substances at the beginning and at the end of a chemical reaction?

	Beginning of a reaction	End of a reaction
A	Elements	Compounds
B	Reactants	Products
C	Solute	Solvent
D	Mixture	Solution

6 The diagram below represents the particles of two different elements which are then mixed but no new substances are formed. Which diagram (A, B or C) best represents the mixture of elements?

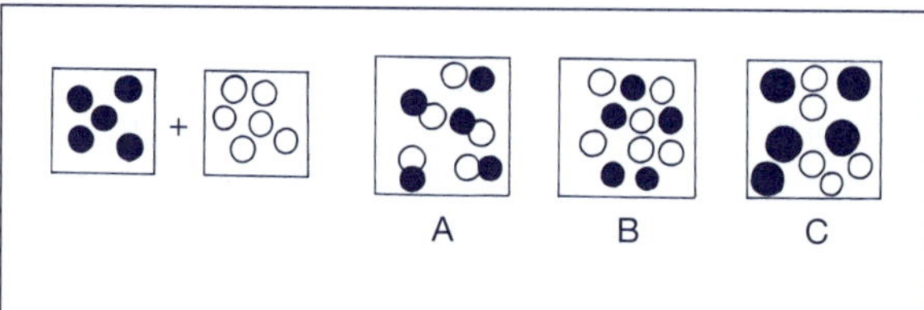

7 Look at the diagram below. When the particles of container A are heated, a chemical reaction takes place. Which of the other containers best represents the particles after the change has taken place?

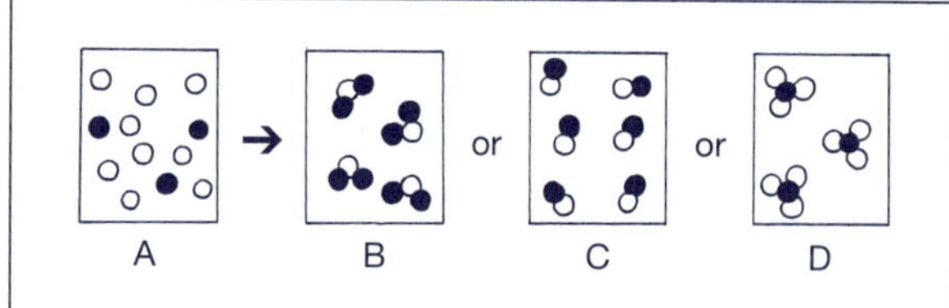

8 Which of the following examples of radiant energy best match with the use or effect of radiant energy?

Radiant energy	Use or effect
A Heat	**1** Taking photographs to see inside the body or inside suitcases at airports
B Light	**2** Cooking and heating
C Radio waves	**3** Cooking and communication
D Microwaves	**4** Radio communication
E Infra-red rays	**5** Causes sunburn of the skin
F Ultra-violet rays	**6** Heating
G X-rays	**7** Allows animals to see

9 Which of the following contains only forces that usually act over a distance?

A collision forces, explosive forces, magnetic forces

B explosive forces, electrical forces, friction

C electrical forces, gravity, magnetic forces

D explosive forces, friction, gravity

10 Which of the following statements about friction are true and which are false?

	Statement	T or F?
A	Friction is always a problem and should be reduced	
B	New tyres give a better grip than old tyres	
C	Making surfaces smooth increases friction between them	
D	Increasing the force between two surface increases the friction	
E	Oil and grease are lubricants that increase friction.	
F	Making the bottom of a canoe smooth helps it move more easily through the water.	
G	Ball bearings help wheels to turn more easily.	
H	A file used to sharpen a bush knife will work better if we put oil or grease on it.	

11 Which of the following are all advantages of simple machines?

I move a small load with a large force
II make things go faster
III change the direction of a force

A I and II only
B II and III only
C I and III only
D I, II and III

12 The passage on the right is a summary of the main ideas of this chapter. Copy and complete the passage in your book. Using the words in the list, find the words that are missing. You can use each word only once.

energy, forces, form, friction, particles, properties, reversible, state, substances, work

Everything is made of matter and all matter is made of tiny ___________. The way that particles are arranged in different kinds of matter affects the ___________ of the matter or the way that the matter behaves. Matter can change and when it changes it will have different properties. When matter changes, the change can be a physical change or a chemical change. Physical changes are usually ___________ and no new substances are formed. A change of ___________ is an example of a physical change. Chemical changes are usually not reversible and new ___________ are formed. Burning is an example of a chemical change.

___________ can exist in many different forms such as heat, light and sound. Energy can change from one ___________ to another. ___________ can be used in everyday life to make things move, to slow them down and to speed them up. The force of ___________ is needed to allow things to move and friction also slow things down, so friction has advantages and disadvantages. Simple machines can do ___________ and make life easier.

4

Earth and beyond

Chapter summary

In this chapter you will have an opportunity to:

- Find out how layers of rock form in the earth
- Find out how fossils form in rocks
- Find out how information is collected that tells us about the way that rock is formed
- Collect samples of rocks
- Look at rock samples to find out about the past
- Make a scale diagram and model of the solar system
- Find out what causes the tides
- Find out about the effects of the movement of the planets, Moon, Sun and stars.

Syllabus references

Strand: Earth and beyond

Sub-strands: Our Earth and its origin
Space exploration

Outcomes: 7.4.1 Collect data of sedimentation process and observe the presence of fossils to explain the living past using a variety of sources, including first-hand experiences.

Investigate the interactions between the Earth, Moon and Sun.

Key facts

- Rock can be formed in different ways. For example, rock can be formed from volcanoes and from the sediments that are carried in water and settle on the bottom of the sea, lakes and swamps.
- The materials that make up rock can move in a cycle. Rock can be slowly weathered or worn away by ice, water and wind, and the small particles can be carried or eroded by water and settle down as sediments. Over thousands of years the sediment can form layers of sedimentary rock.
- When plants and animals die they can become buried with the sediments and form fossils.
- Fossils are the preserved remains or traces of plants and animals that lived millions of years ago.
- Fossils can be used to work out how long ago a rock was formed and what plants and animals were living at that time.
- Our solar system consists of eight planets, together with their moons, dwarf planets, asteroids, meteors and comets.
- We can observe changes in the position of the planets, the Moon and the Sun and these changes affect our way of life.
- The tilt of the Earth towards the Sun and the movement of the Earth around the Sun affects the length of day and night and the change of the seasons.
- The position of the Earth, Moon and Sun causes tides.

Our Earth and its origin

The formation of rocks

Igneous rocks

The first rocks formed on the Earth when the molten rock or **magma** inside the Earth began to cool down. The molten rock that comes out of a volcano is called lava and it forms rocks when it cools. These rocks are called **igneous rocks** and are usually very hard. Papua New Guinea has many volcanoes, so there are many igneous rocks such as **basalt**, **granite** and **andesite**. Basalt rocks can be seen near Sogeri, Lae and Mount Hagen and many other places in Papua New Guinea.

Basalt rocks

Obsidian is another igneous rock that is formed when the lava from a volcano cools quickly in water. Obsidian looks like black glass and can be made into tools with a sharp edge. Obsidian from Lou Island in Manus Province was traded widely in the south west Pacific and used to make spears, scrapers and other sharp tools.

Obsidian tools found on Lou Island and other parts of Manus Province are over 2000 years old.

However, some igneous rocks are not hard. For example, the **pumice** that comes out of volcanoes has many holes in it that are formed by bubbles of gas in the rock. Pumice is so light that it can float on water. When the volcanoes erupted in Rabaul in September 1994, Simpson harbour was covered in pumice.

Pumice floating on the water after the volcanic eruption in Rabaul, in September 1994.

Sedimentary rocks

Small pieces of clay, silt and fine sand are worn away from the rocks and carried by rivers into lakes and to the sea. When the river reaches the sea or lake, the water slows down and the material being carried in the water falls to the sea floor. This material is called **sediment**. Over thousands of years, layers of sediments can build up and may form new rocks called **sedimentary rocks**. Sandstone, mudstone, conglomerate and limestone are examples of sedimentary rock.

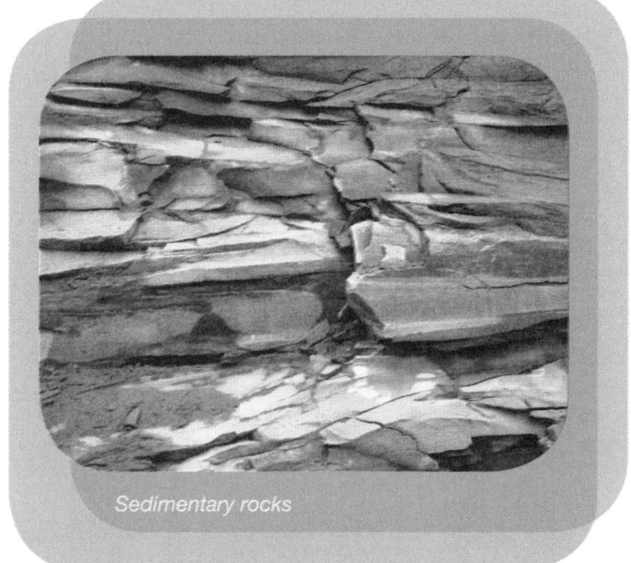
Sedimentary rocks

The formation of sedimentary rocks

Sedimentary rock often has layers. When sedimentary rocks are formed, the remains of plants and animals may be trapped in the layers. These remains become part of the rock and are called **fossils**. Fossils can be used to work out the age of the rock and tell what the weather was like in the past, so they help us to understand the history of the Earth. Fossils are often found in Papua New Guinea. For example, the limestone in the highlands is made up of fossilised coral reefs.

Stalactites and stalagmites

A fossil

Limestone can be dissolved by rain and caves can be formed. Limestone caves often have stalactites and stalagmites, which are formed from dripping water and are also known as dripstone.

Metamorphic rocks

Igneous and sedimentary rocks deep within the Earth's **crust** are under high pressures and temperatures, which usually make the rocks harder and make them look different from each other. Rocks that are formed in this way are called **metamorphic rocks** because they have been changed. Slate is an example of metamorphic rock. The layers in slate are so well formed that it can be split into sheets. These split sheets can be used as tiles for roofs and floors. Slate is also used to make pool tables because a big sheet of slate is flat and smooth. Marble is another metamorphic rock that can be used to make floors and statues. The floor of the National Parliament in Port Moresby is made from marble.

A marble statue

Slate used on a roof.

Weathering and erosion

All things are being slowly worn down. For example, concrete buildings, bridges and pavement sometimes start to break up into smaller pieces. The paverment at Ela Beach in Port Moresby that was new in the 1980s started to break up after about ten years due to the salt spray from the sea.

All rocks are slowly worn down into smaller pieces by the sun, wind, rain and temperature. This process, called **weathering**, goes on all the time. For example, rocks can become very hot in the daytime and then get cold at night. These changes in temperature can make the rocks expand and contract and the surface of the rocks begin to break into smaller pieces.

In high mountains the temperature can fall below 0°C at night. Water in small cracks in the rock will freeze and turn to ice. Water expands when it freezes and the force is big enough to make the crack a little bit wider. Over a long period of time the crack will gradually become bigger and bigger and eventually a small piece of rock breaks off.

Plant roots can also grow into rocks and this causes the rocks to crack and break into smaller pieces.

Plants growing on rocks can help to break them into smaller pieces.

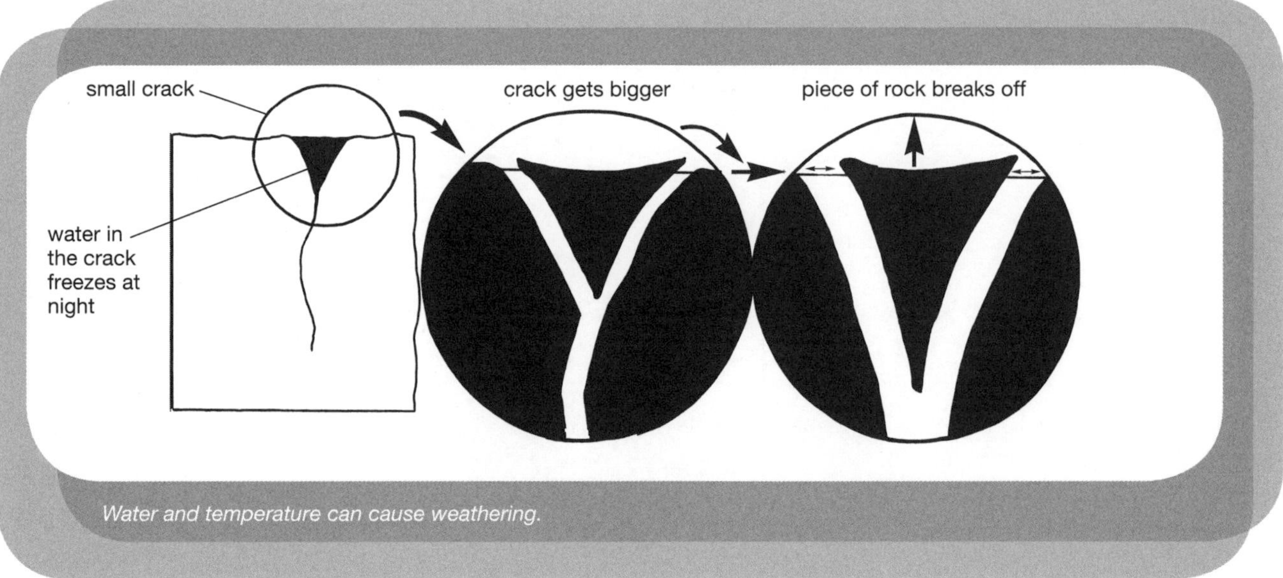

Water and temperature can cause weathering.

Running water is the main cause of erosion.

The small pieces of material that come from the weathering of rocks and soil may be carried away by water and wind. This process is called erosion. Large amounts of material can be carried in this way. Running water is the main cause of erosion in Papua New Guinea.

When a river looks muddy, it is carrying tiny pieces of rock in **suspension**. This suspended material includes clay, silt and fine sand. These substances cannot settle because the water is always moving or **turbulent**.

When there is a flood there is a greater flow of water so that sand, pebbles or small stones and boulders roll or slide along the river bed.

In some countries the rocks in mountains are worn away by slow moving rivers of ice called **glaciers**. The rocks touching the ice are slowly eroded and this makes rock 'flour'. When the ice melts, the rock flour is carried in the water and forms a river that looks cloudy. For example, the rivers that run from the glaciers in New Zealand are usually cloudy because of the rock flour in the water.

Although weathering and erosion take place all the time, in some places the land is being pushed up to form mountains. This proces, called **uplift**, is the way in which the mountains were formed in Papua New Guinea. These high areas of land are again weathered and eroded and the process continues.

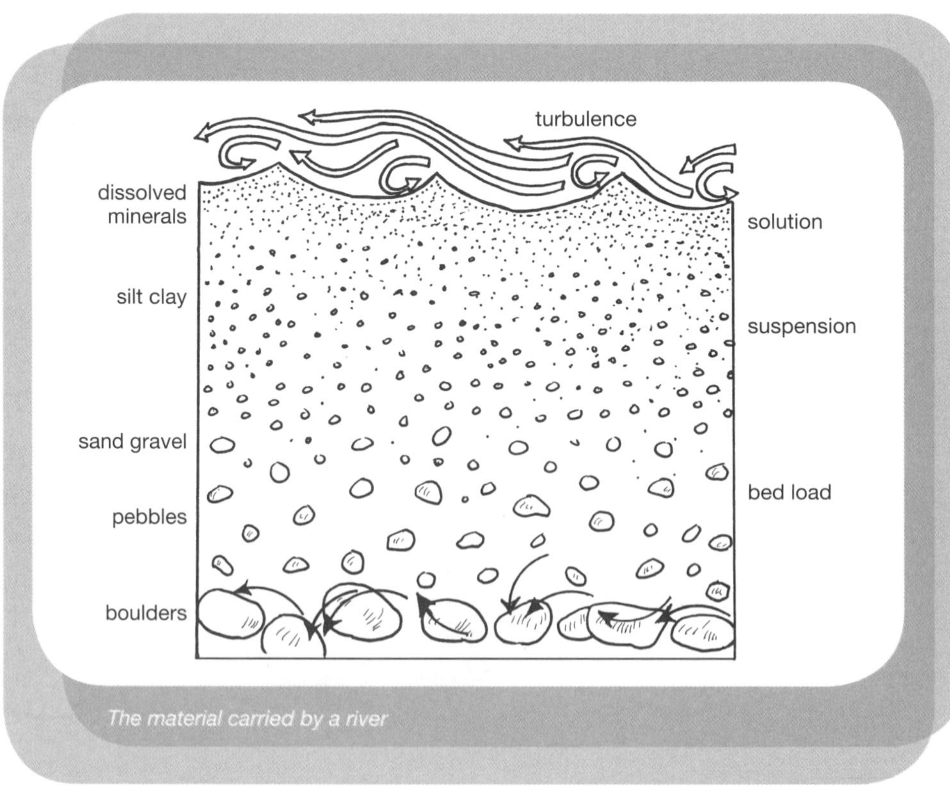

The material carried by a river

The action of weathering and erosion also produces soils that can support plants. Plants provide the basic source of food for all animals. When plants and animals die, some of the materials taken from the soil will be returned to the earth.

The rock cycle

All of the processes of rock formation, uplift, weathering and erosion that occur in the Earth's crust are part of the **rock cycle**.

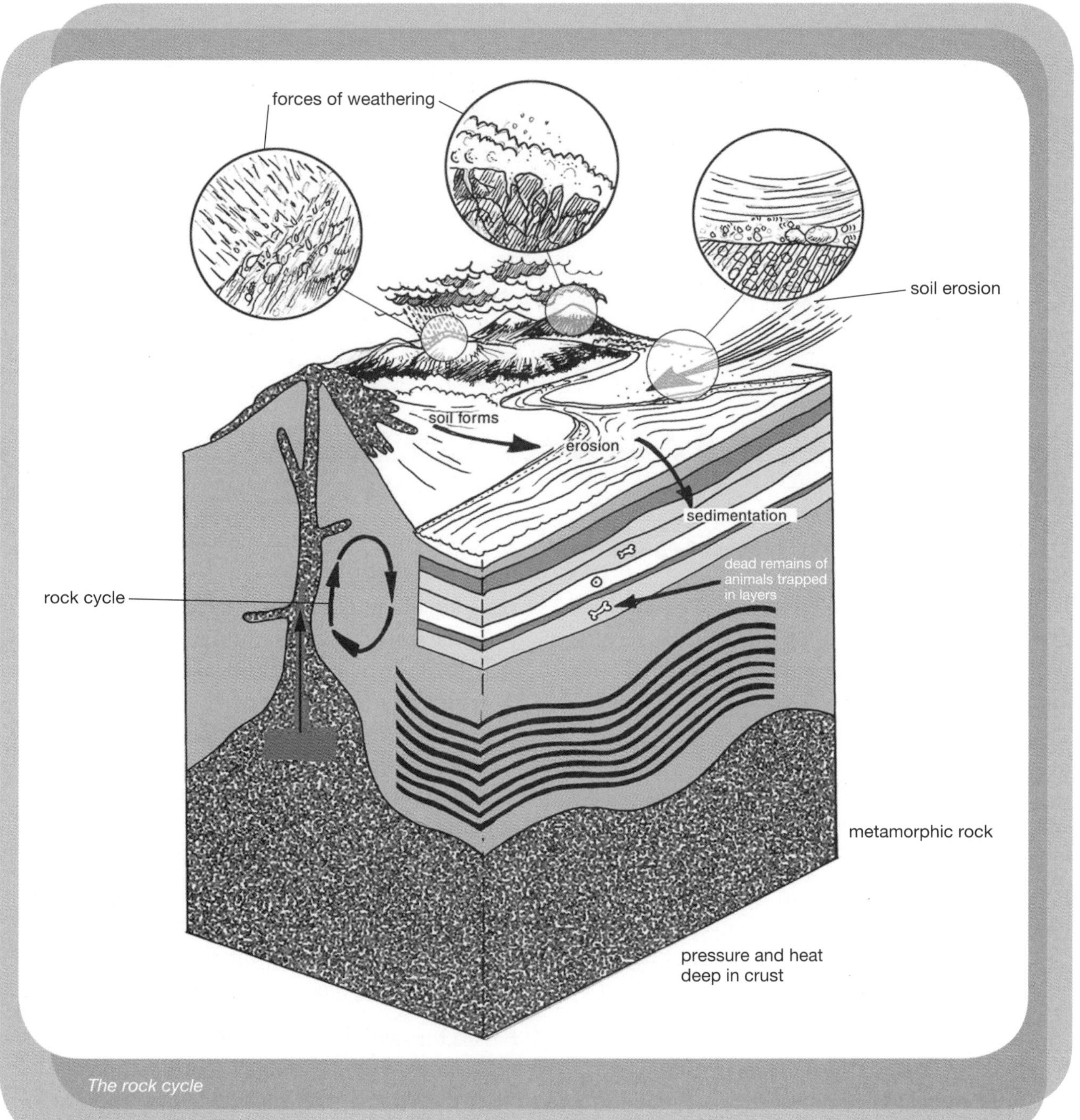

The rock cycle

For you to try

1 **Investigation: Weathering**

a Collect a small piece of sandstone rock, a piece of fencing wire, an empty tin, a funnel made from a plastic bottle, a piece of newspaper, and a magnifying glass.

b Fix the small piece of sandstone in one end of the fencing wire.

c Heat the sandstone in the flames of a fire for a minute or two using the wire as a holder. The wire must be long enough so that you do not burn yourself.

d Dip the hot rock into a tin of water. Everyone should keep well away from the tin when you do this in case the hot rock splits.

e Repeat this process of heating and cooling at least three times.

f Place a piece of newspaper in the funnel and filter the water from the tin.

g Remove the paper filter, allow it to dry and observe the tiny pieces of rock.

h Explain what you did and what you found out.

i Draw diagrams to show the shape of the rock before and after heating.

How fossils are formed

Fossils are the remains or evidence of living things that have been preserved, usually in rock. Fossils can be formed in several ways but will form only under special conditions.

1 Mineralisation

The hard parts of plants and animals can form fossils as follows:

- After they died, some animals were quickly buried by sinking in mud or sediment in the sea or in a lake or river. Animlas that were not buried quickly would have been eaten by scavengers.
- The hard parts of the animals that didn't rot, like bones and teeth, were covered in the newly-formed sediment.
- Over time, more and more sediment covered the remains of the animal.
- After a long time, the chemicals in the buried parts slowly changed. Substances in the bone, called minerals, dissolved and were replaced with minerals from the water and sediment that had soaked in. Other minerals sometimes filled up the spaces and the minerals sometimes changed their structure after many years.
- This process, called **mineralisation**, results in a copy of the original object that looks like rock. So fossils are made of different substances and have a different colour than the original object.

Fossils formed in this way are not common because most of the animals that die just rot away. Also, the sedimentary rocks in which these fossils form must be lifted up and then weathered before they can be found. Finding fossils is like finding just a few pages that have been torn from an old book, and on the page we can read only a few words.

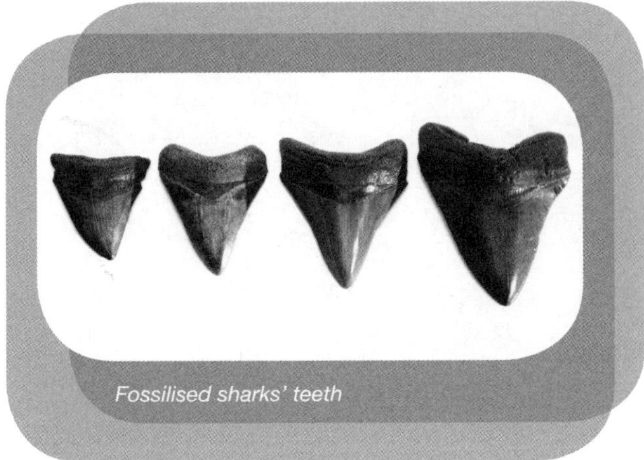

Fossilised sharks' teeth

2 Moulds and casts

Sometimes organisms became buried or trapped in mud, clay or ash from a volcano, which later hardened around them. When the bodies decay they leave a mould that shows the shape of the original. The mould that is formed can be external or internal. The external mould is created when the bodies dissolve and leave an empty space that is imprinted with the details of the outside of the organisms. Internal moulds form inside hollow structures when the interior of an organism is filled with another material, which makes a cast. This can happen with shellfish; when the shell disappears, an impression of the interior is left in the cast.

A fossil of a shell that has become an external mould. The external details of the shell can be seen in the cavity.

Internal mould of a seashell

3 Impressions

An impression is an **imprint** or shape left behind by an organism. Impressions may be of plants or animals themselves, or of tracks or footprints left by animals. Most impressions are found in sediment such as clay or silt. Impressions are preserved when the soft mud or sediment in which they are made hardens into rock.

Impressions of plants often show the veins of the leaves, and animal impressions sometimes show the skeleton. Footprints or other tracks can tell us about the size of the animal and the way that it moved.

A fossil showing the impression of a plant

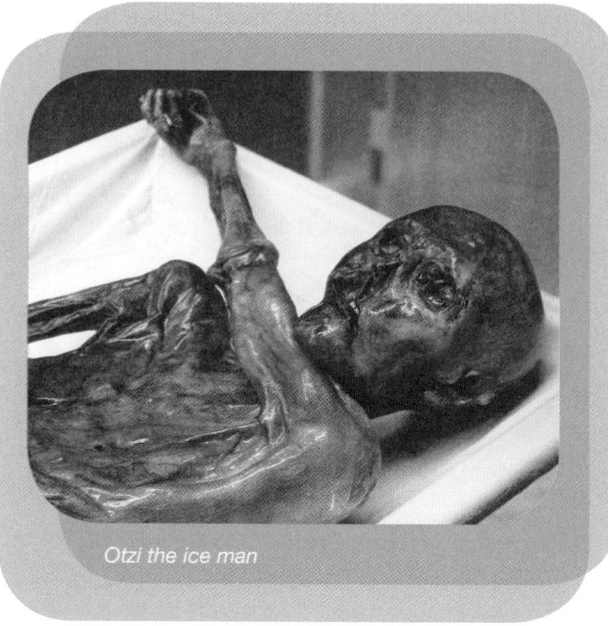
Otzi the ice man

Other kinds of fossils

Most fossils are found in rocks but they have also been found in **amber**, **coal** and ice.

Amber is the fossilised gum from a type of pine tree. Insects and seeds were sometimes caught in the sticky gum. When the gum sets hard, some of the insects and seeds can be preserved for millions of years. Living things do not decay when they are covered with amber because air cannot reach them.

Coal is a hard black substance that is formed underground from plants and animals that lived thousands of years ago. Coal often contains fossils.

Ice is another good way to preserve living things, because they do not decay. In 1991, a fossilised human being was found in the mountains on the border between Austria and Italy, together with his clothes made from animal skins and his axe and arrows. Scientists have worked out that he lived 5300 years ago and have called him Otzi after the area in which he was found. Otzi is the oldest and best preserved fossil of this kind.

Sometimes limestone caves contain fossils of land animals. The animals may have fallen into the cave and the conditions in the cave have helped to preserve the remains. Many of the fossils of human beings that lived thousands of years ago have been found in caves.

Fossil fuels

Coal, oil and natural gas are the remains of plants and animals that lived thousands of years ago and are known as **fossil fuels** because they can be burned to give energy. Oil and natural gas are both found in Papua New Guinea. Fossil fuels are the most important source of energy used in the world today. Because fossil fuels cannot be replaced they are described as a **non-renewable** resource.

For you to try

1 **Investigation: Collecting sediments**

a Collect the tube from the inside of a toilet roll, a piece of newspaper and different types of mud, fine soil or sediment, each with a different colour (at least three different types), in a tin.

b Squash the piece of newspaper into a ball and push it into one end of the tube to close off the bottom of the tube.

c Add enough water to each tin of soil and stir well to make a thick mud that will pour easily.

d Pour one mud into the cardboard tube and carefully shake the tube to help it to settle. It doesn't matter if a little mud runs out of the tube, but hold your hand over the end to stop the squashed newspaper from coming out.

e Repeat with the other types of mud. Each mud should take up about an equal part of the space inside the tube.

f Place the tube in the sun for several days so that it will dry out. Do not let the tube get wet.

g When it is dry and strong enough, carefully peel off the cardboard tube from the tube of mud.

h Observe and draw a labelled diagram of the sediments.

2 **Investigation: Making sedimentary rocks with fossils**

a Collect some sand, gravel, soil with sticks and leaves removed or very fine silt, crushed lime, Plaster of Paris, seashells or pieces of shell, small fish bones, old Tetrapak drink containers (250 mL), old tins or jars (for mixing plaster), and fine sandpaper.

b In groups choose a type of rock to make from the table on page 120. Each group should choose a different type of rock.

c In the table, find the type of sediment that forms that type of rock and the fossils that you might find in that environment.

d Add this sediment to the empty drink container and the fossils.

e Mix some Plaster of Paris and add this to the drink container to cement the sediment and remains together.

f When the plaster has set, tear off the drink container and gently rub the outside with fine sandpaper.

g Observe the rock that you have made and draw a labelled diagram.

h Observe the other types of rock that other groups have made and discuss the differences.

i Draw labelled diagrams of the other kinds of rocks.

Making sedimentary rocks			
Environment	**Type of sediment**	**Fossils you might find there**	**Rock type produced**
River	Pebbles	Fish, plants	Conglomerate rock
Beach	Sandy	Shells, seaweed	Sandstone
Bottom of the shallow sea	Mud or silt	Shells fish	Shale
Bottom of the deep sea	Crushed white lime	Few shells, fish	Limestone

Using fossils

Scientists think that the Earth is about 5000 million years old. Fossil plants and animals appeared in large numbers about 300 million years ago, and human beings have developed in the last three million years.

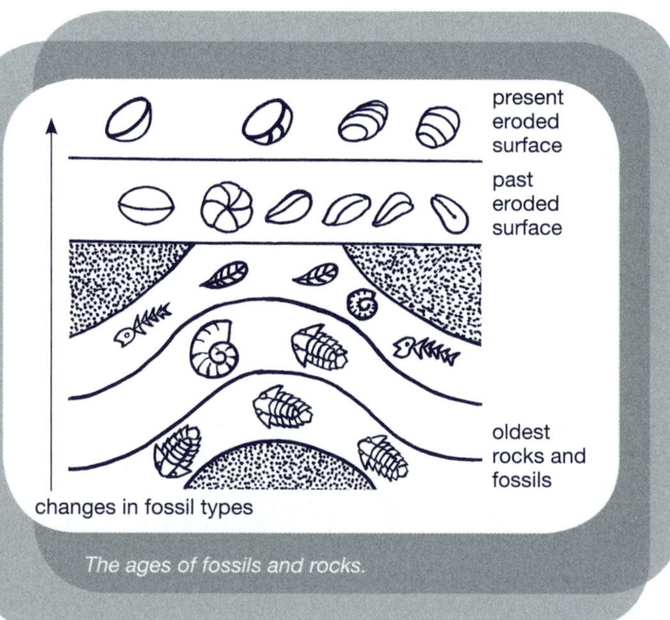

The ages of fossils and rocks.

Fossils found in sedimentary rocks help scientists to find out about the past. Over a period of time, animals slowly change from a simple to a more complex form. This means that some fossils may have lived on the Earth for only a few million years, which is a short time in the history of the Earth. So these fossil animals are very useful to work out the age of the rock in which they are found. Fossils of these animals are called **index fossils** because we can use them like the index at the back of a book to find information about other living things and the time when they lived.

Sediments are deposited gradually in layers so the older layers will be at the bottom with the younger rocks on top. The fossils found in the rocks will prove this, as the older, simpler fossils will be at the bottom. Fossils can be used to show which animals and plants lived at the same time and which rocks are older or younger than other rocks.

In some parts of the world, the movement of the earth has changed this pattern and old rocks may cover younger rocks. Fossils are used to work out the ages of these rocks. If the rocks have been turned upside down, the older fossils will now be found in the top layers of rocks.

Space exploration

The universe

The whole of space, all the stars and planets, and everything else in space is called the universe. Scientists think that billions of years ago all the matter and energy in the universe was very hot and tightly squashed together, and that about 14 billion years ago there was a big explosion that started to expand or spread out. This is called the **Big Bang** theory.

- The Milky Way is the bright band of light that stretches across the sky.
- The glow comes from millions of individual stars that are too faint to be seen with the naked eye.
- The Sun is one of about 100 000 stars in our galaxy.
- Our Sun lies in one of the spiral arms towards the edge of our galaxy.

Some of the most interesting objects in the universe are the **galaxies**.

- Galaxies are very large groups of millions of stars.
- Seen from above, some galaxies look like spirals with arms spreading out from the centre. Seen from the side galaxies are usually flat and disc-shaped.
- Galaxies are separated by very large distances.
- We live in a galaxy that has a spiral shape. It is called the **Milky Way** galaxy.

A spiral galaxy much like our own

- The Andromeda galaxy is one of our nearest galaxies. It is part of the group of galaxies to which our Milky Way galaxy belongs.

The solar system

Our **solar system** is made up of the Sun and a family of eight planets, together with many moons and **asteroids**. The Sun is at the centre of our solar system and the planets revolve around it. The planets revolve around the Sun like marbles rolling around in a big dish or bowl. The other members of the solar system are dwarf planets, **comets** and **meteors**.

The eight planets in the solar system, beginning with the nearest to the Sun, are Mercury, Venus, Earth, Mars, Jupiter, Saturn, Uranus and Neptune.

Pluto is beyond Neptune and was included as the ninth planet for many years. However, in 2006 a group of scientists made a new definition of a planet. This means that Pluto is no longer a planet but is described as a dwarf planet, together with Eris and Ceres. This is also an example of the way in which scientists are ready to change their ideas to explain their observations.

On a cloudless night one or two of the planets can usually be seen shining in the sky. Planets are hard to tell apart from the stars, but unlike the stars they do not give out their own light. Planets reflect light from the Sun and do not twinkle like stars but seem to give a steady light.

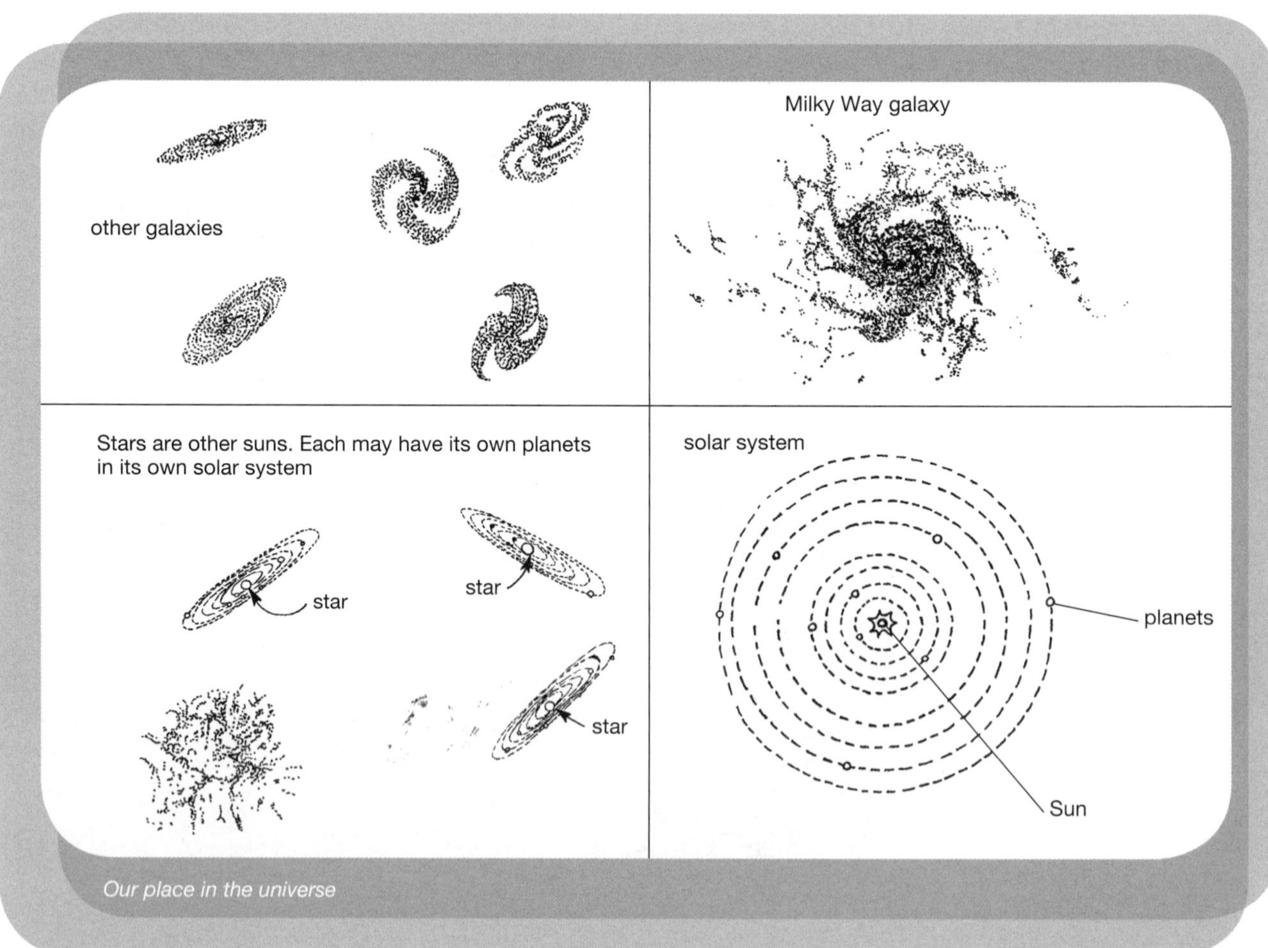

Our place in the universe

The position of our solar system in one of the spiral arms of our Milky Way galaxy

Comets

Comets are pieces of rock and ice that orbit the Sun, but their path is not like those of the planets. Most comets spend much of their time way out beyond Pluto and make regular swoops back into the solar system and around the Sun. As a comet approaches the Sun, it warms up and some of its gases evaporate. The energy from the Sun pushes this gas away, causing it to glow brightly and form a long, shining tail.

Planets also seem to move among the stars from night to night. The word *planet* means wanderer. Long ago people noticed that while stars kept to their patterns, the planets move slowly across the sky.

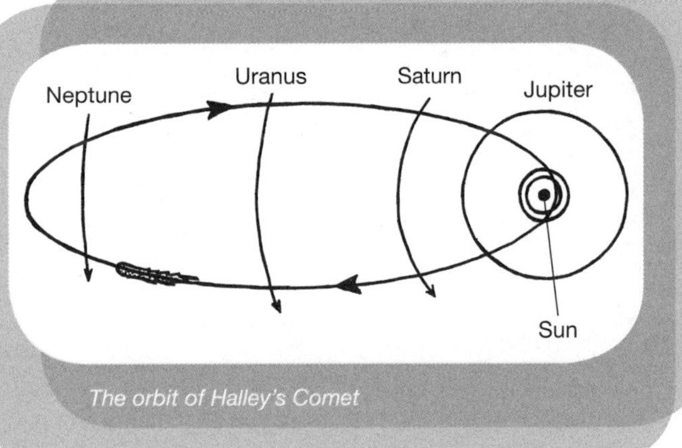

The orbit of Halley's Comet

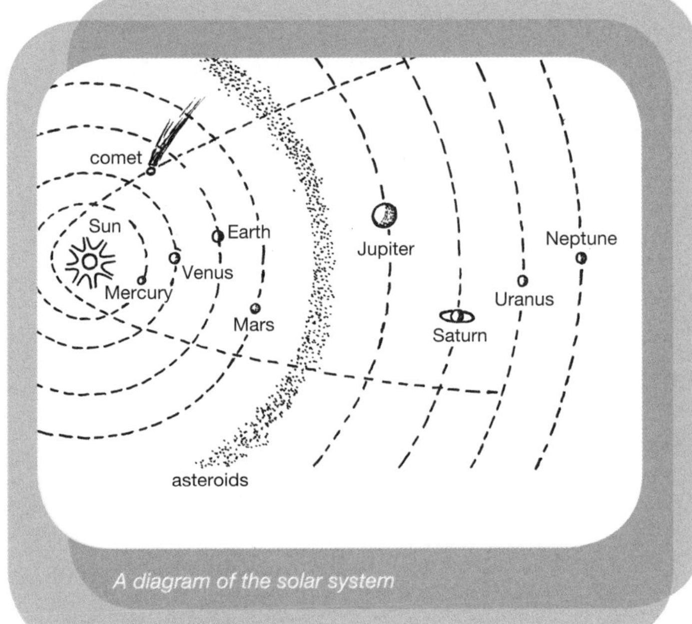

A diagram of the solar system

The most famous comet is called Halley's Comet, which returns to the solar system every 76 years. Since 87 BC, people have observed and recorded Halley's Comet each time it has come close to the Earth. Halley's Comet returned to the Earth in late 1985 and early 1986 and was visible while it turned around the Sun. It will not be seen again until it returns in 2061.

Scientists sent five spacecraft to study Halley's Comet as it passed the Sun in March 1986. They found that the comet has a solid central part, about 15 kilometres long and 10 kilometres wide. This means that it is a bit smaller than Karkar Island in

Halley's Comet

Madang Province. The comet's centre is rough, with hills, hollows and **craters**. It is very dark and hardly any light is reflected from it. Fast jets of water vapour and dust come from this centre as it is heated by the Sun. Every second, many tonnes of gas and a few tonnes of dust are produced, which make up the tail of the comet.

Meteors

Apart from the planets, dwarf planets, asteroids and comets, which all have certain paths around the Sun, there are many wandering pieces of matter in the solar system called meteors. Most of them burn up when they enter the Earth's atmosphere, leaving fiery tails called **shooting stars** or **falling stars**. A few of the larger meteors do reach the Earth's surface and these are called **meteorites**. When a large meteorite hits the Earth it can leave a mark called a crater.

In March 1975, a small meteorite landed near Goroka. This piece of rock measured 18 centimetres in diameter and weighed 7.33 kilograms. It was called the Ijopega meteorite, after the local place name.

A meteorite crater

Asteroid belt

Between Mars and Jupiter is a belt of widely separated lumps of rock called **asteroids**. Scientists believe that the asteroids are pieces of material that did not have the opportunity to form a planet, rather than the remains of a planet that has broken up. Hundreds of thousands of asteroids have been discovered but only sixteen have a diameter of 240 km or greater. Some are the size of small stones.

The planets

The table below gives a comparison of the planets.

Planet	Summary
Mercury	The smallest and hottest planet
Venus	The same size as the Earth and covered with thick clouds; also known as the morning star and the evening star, and is often the brightest object in the sky
Earth	The planet on which we live
Mars	The red planet, smaller than the Earth, with two polar ice caps; its surface is covered with craters
Jupiter	The largest planet made mainly of gases; it has a prominent red spot
Saturn	The ringed planet; it is the second largest planet
Uranus	Bigger than the Earth, with an axis on its side; it has thin rings
Neptune	Bigger than the Earth and is very cold

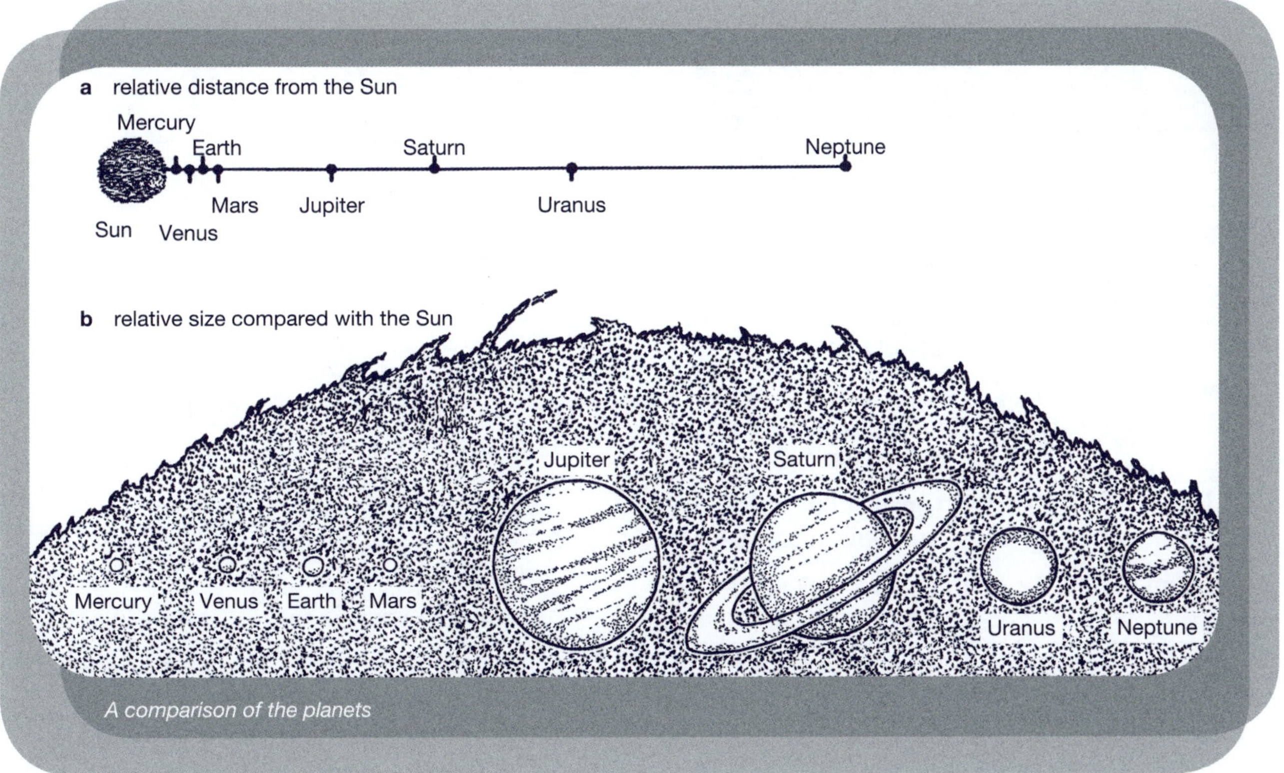

A comparison of the planets

For you to try

1 Investigation: Making a model solar system

a Collect a large sheet of paper and a selection of the common objects described in the table below, or similar objects, and some glue.

b Using the diagrams of the solar system in this chapter, draw the orbits of the planets on the sheet of paper.

c Using the common objects that you have collected, arrange them in order to represent the planets in a model of the solar system.

d Label each planet and give your model a heading or title.

e Show your model to other groups and display it for visitors to see.

Planet	Size for model	Common object of same size
Mercury	2.1 mm	half a grain of white rice or a pin head
Venus	5.3 mm	seed or small polystyrene ball
Earth	5.5 mm	seed or small polystyrene ball
Mars	3.0 mm	grain of rice or pin with plastic, coloured ball on the end
Jupiter	62.0 mm	lemon or ball made from woven pandanus
Saturn	52.0 mm	lemon or ball made from woven pandanus
Uranus	24.2 mm	large glass marble
Neptune	20.8 mm	large glass marble

2 Investigation: How far apart are the planets?

a Collect nine pieces of paper and write the name of each planet on a piece of paper. Write 'Sun' on the ninth piece of paper.

b Give each piece of paper to one student.

c Go outside and ask the nine students with labels to stand apart according to the distances shown in the table below.

Planet	Distance from model Sun	
Mercury	0.58 m	¾ pace
Venus	1.08 m	¼ pace
Earth	1.50 m	2 paces
Mars	2.28 m	3 paces
Jupiter	7.78 m	10 paces
Saturn	14.27 m	18 paces
Uranus	28.70 m	36 paces
Neptune	44. 97 m	56 paces

3 Which planets are smallest and largest?

4 Which planets are closest and furthest from the Sun?

The origin of the Earth

People in Papua New Guinea often have stories that explain how the Earth was formed or how a particular mountain, river, lake or cave was formed. These stories are called **creation stories**.

Scientists also have explanations of how the Earth was created. Scientists think that the Earth formed from a large cloud of very hot dust and gas around the Sun about 4600 million years ago. As the gases and dust cooled, the Earth formed. It gradually became smaller to form a ball-shape of molten rock with a solid surface. The Earth has been cooling for millions of years, but the inside is still very hot.

The Earth's motion

The Earth is a satellite of the Sun. This means that the Earth orbits or travels around the Sun. The Earth acts as if there is a string between it and the Sun.

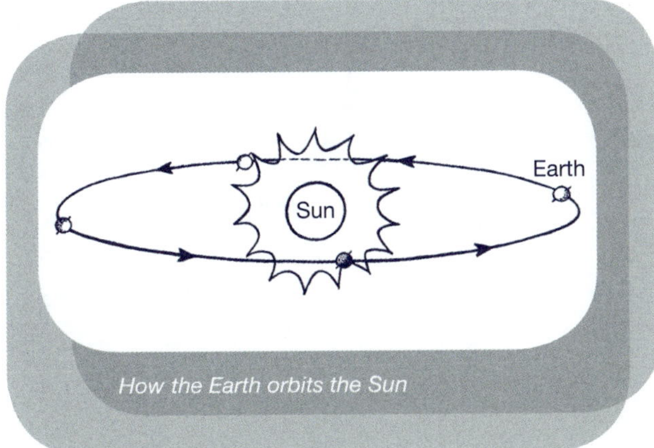

How the Earth orbits the Sun

The time taken for the Earth to orbit once around the Sun is called a year, which is equal to 365¼ days. To make things easier, we say that a year has 365 days. However, every four years, an extra day is added to the month of February, so that year has 366 days. This is called a leap year.

The movement of the Earth around the Sun causes the seasons, changes in the direction of the wind, and the movement of the position where the Sun rises and sets on the horizon.

Night and day

At any time, only half the Earth is in sunlight, while the other half is in shadow. The half that is brightly lit is in daytime and the half that is in darkness is in night-time.

The Earth spins around an imaginary line through its centre, which is called its **axis**. The spinning of the Earth on its axis is called its **rotation**. As the Earth spins or rotates in an anti-clockwise direction, the darkened parts move from darkness to light and into darkness again.

The Earth spins or rotates once every twenty-four hours. People who live close to the equator, like in Papua New Guinea, have twelve hours of daylight and twelve hours of darkness. People who live further away from the equator have different lengths of day and night.

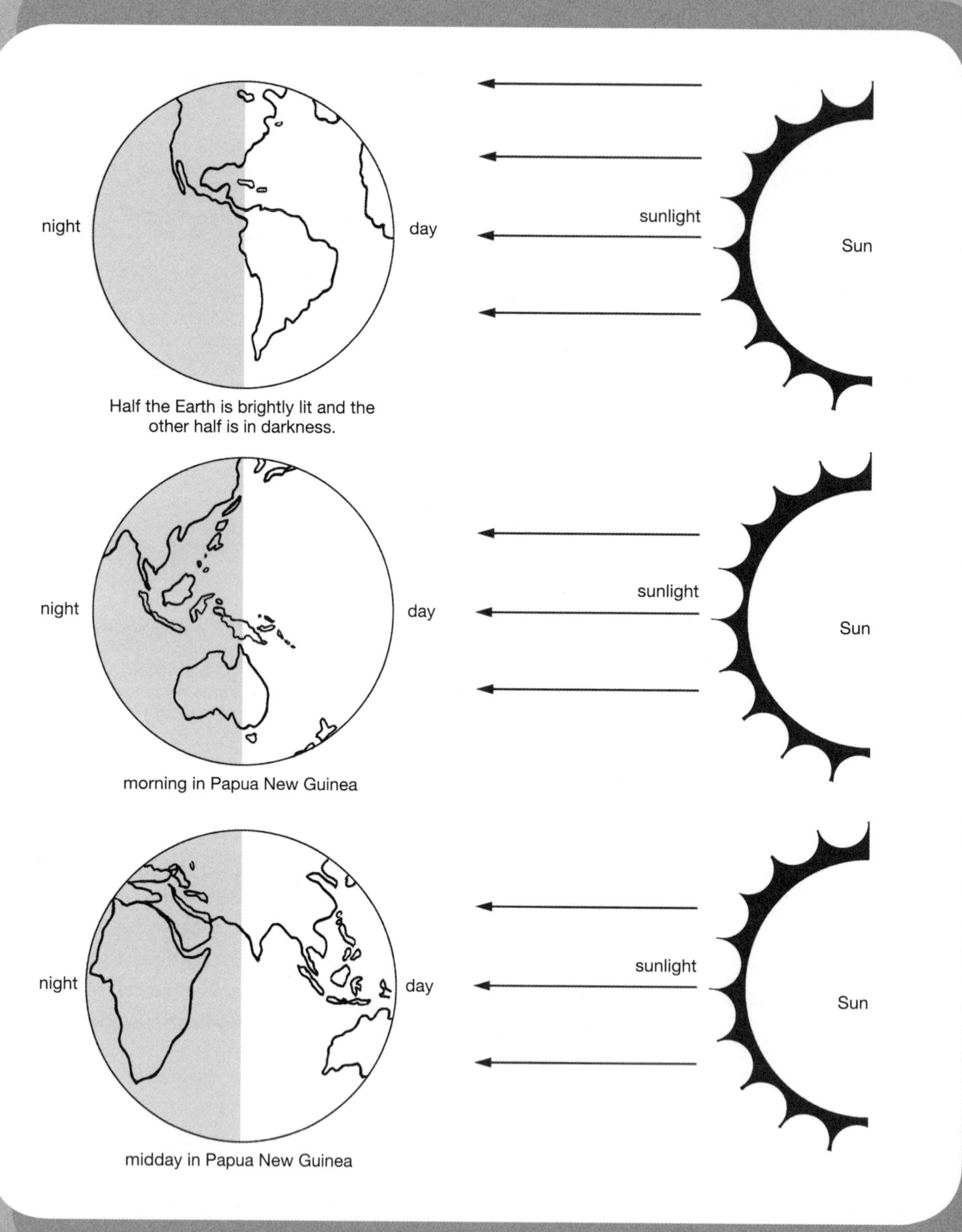

Night and day

Seasons

The axis of the Earth is tilted towards the Sun, which causes the seasons. People who live in countries a long way north or south of the equator have four different seasons depending on the hemisphere in which they live and the time of the year. Different seasons can have very different temperatures as well as different day lengths. The seasons are called spring, summer, autumn and winter. When it is summer in the southern hemisphere it is winter in the northern hemisphere. The seasons in different parts of the world are summarised in the table. Summer is the hottest season because that part of the world is tilted more closely to the Sun.

Months	Countries	Season	Temperature	Length of day and night
December, January, February	Australia and New Zealand (southern hemisphere)	Summer	Warm or hot	Long days and short nights
	Europe, USA, Canada (northern hemisphere)	Winter	Cold—may have frost, snow and ice	Short days and long nights
June, July, August	Australia and New Zealand (southern hemisphere)	Winter	Cold—may mean frost, snow and ice	Short days and long nights
	Europe, USA, Canada (northern hemisphere)	Summer	Warm or hot	Long days and short nights

For you to try

1 **Investigation: Night and day**

a Collect a torch and a large ball or balloon as a model of the Earth (globe).

b Draw the continents on to the ball or balloon.

c Make the room as dark as possible and shine the torch onto the model of the Earth. The torch takes the place of the Sun.

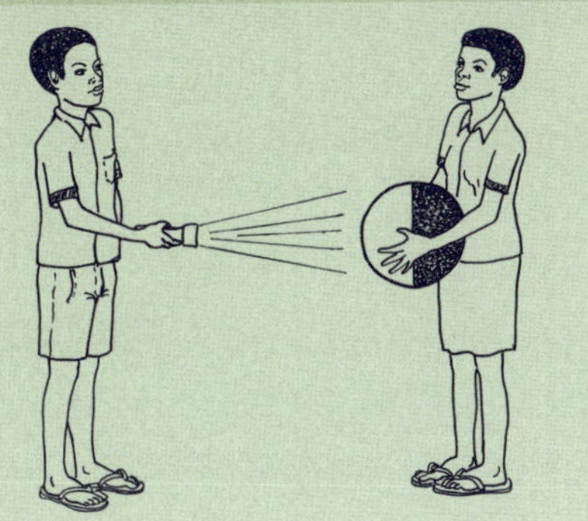

d It is daytime on the part of the Earth with the light shining on it, and it is night on the part of the Earth in shadow.

e Rotate the Earth so that dawn, then dusk, then dawn appears.

f In which direction does the Earth spin?

2 **Investigation: One year and the seasons**

a Collect a pressure lamp or electric lamp and a large ball or balloon as a model of the Earth (globe).

b Draw the continents on to the ball or balloon.

c Make the room as dark as possible and put the lamp on a chair or stool in the middle of the room to represent the Sun.

d Do the following two investigations:

I **One year**

a Hold the model of the Earth and walk in a circle around the pressure lamp. This represents the Earth moving around the Sun. One circle or one orbit is one year.

b To make it a true model, you should spin the Earth anti-clockwise as it rotates around the Sun. How many times does the Earth spin as it makes one orbit around the Sun?

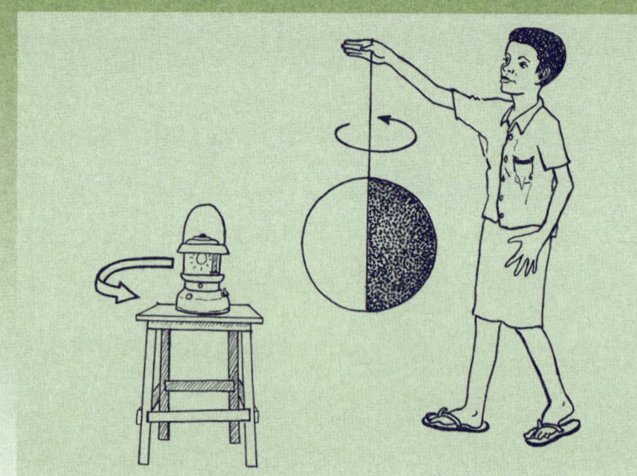

II The seasons

a Since the Earth is tilted, hold your model Earth so that it is slightly tilted. Do not change the angle of this tilt during the experiment.

b Walk slowly in a circle around the lamp, moving the model Earth so that it always faces the lamp. Make sure the tilt always points in the same direction.

c The Earth on the right-hand side of the diagram shows the position in summer in Australia. Notice that the Sun appears to be overhead in the southern hemisphere.

d Walk half a circle around the Sun and again stop and look at the model of the Earth. How is it different? Which part of the Earth is having summer?

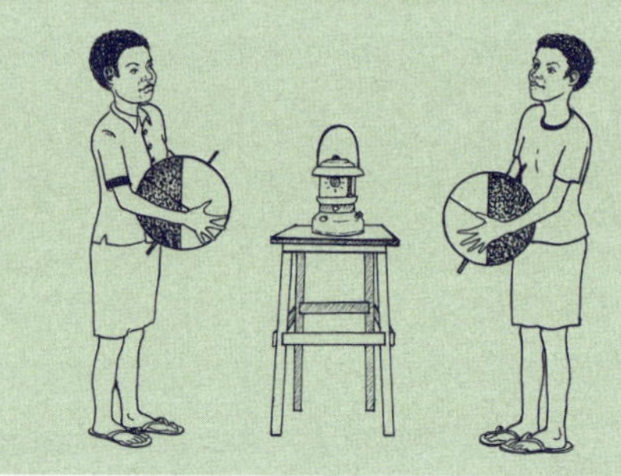

The Earth's moon

- The Moon is the only natural satellite of the Earth.
- It is 384 000 km from the Earth and its diameter is 3476 km, about a quarter of the diameter of the Earth.
- The Moon spins or rotates once in exactly the time it takes to orbit the Earth, which is about 28 days. This means that the same side of the Moon is always seen from the Earth. This side is called the near side and the opposite side is called the far side.
- The Moon rises and sets just like the Sun. It rises about 50 minutes later each day.
- The Moon is in the sky during the day as well as the night but it is harder to see.
- The Moon has a weak gravity, which is about one sixth that of the Earth.
- The temperature on the Moon varies from minus 170°C to 130°C. The Moon has no atmosphere or weather, but may have some ice.
- The Moon has been hit by many meteorites and the surface has about half a million craters.

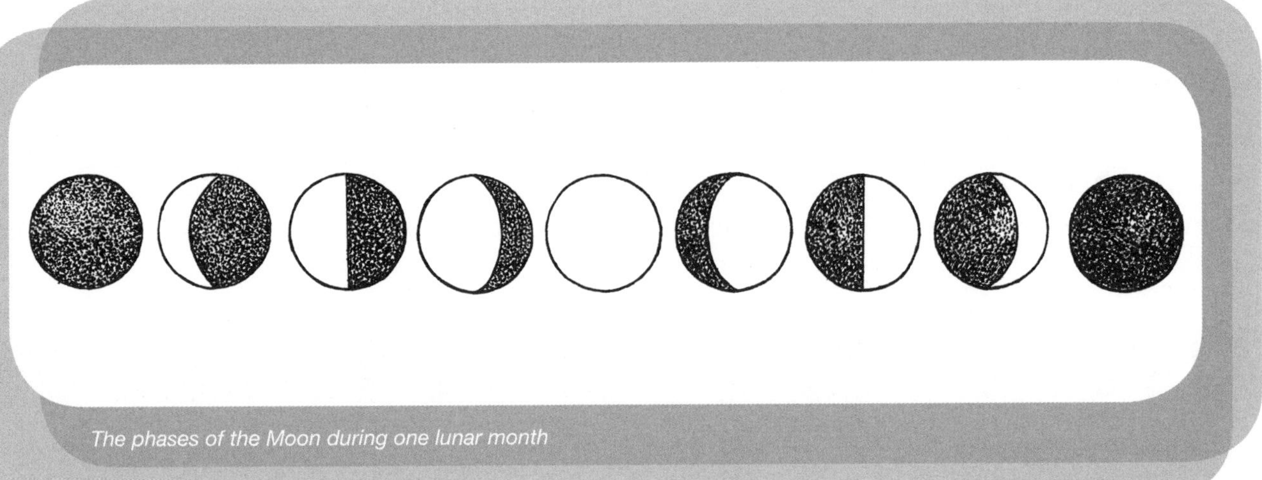
The phases of the Moon during one lunar month

- The Moon is covered with rocks, boulders and dark soil.
- Neil Armstrong and Edwin 'Buzz' Aldrin were the first people to walk on the Moon in July, 1969. Twelve astronauts have now walked on the Moon and brought back about 200 samples of Moon rock.

Phases of the Moon

The changes in the appearance of the moon are called the **phases of the Moon**. The Moon is always round and does not change its shape. What changes is the amount of the Moon that we can see from the Earth because it is lit by the Sun. This depends on the positions of the Earth, Moon and Sun. A **lunar month** lasts for 28 days, and in this time the Moon goes through a cycle of light and dark shapes. The different phases of the Moon during one lunar month are shown in the diagram at the top of this page.

There are thirteen lunar months each year. The lunar calendar is used to set the time for events such as Easter, Chinese New Year, and Ramadan, which is one month each year when Muslim people do not eat or drink from sunrise to sunset each day.

Tides

People who live near the sea or travel on boats know that the sea rises and falls at different times of the day and night. These changes in the level of the sea are called tides and are caused by the gravitational pull of the Moon on the Earth. As the Earth rotates, there are two cycles of high and low tides, about thirteen hours apart.

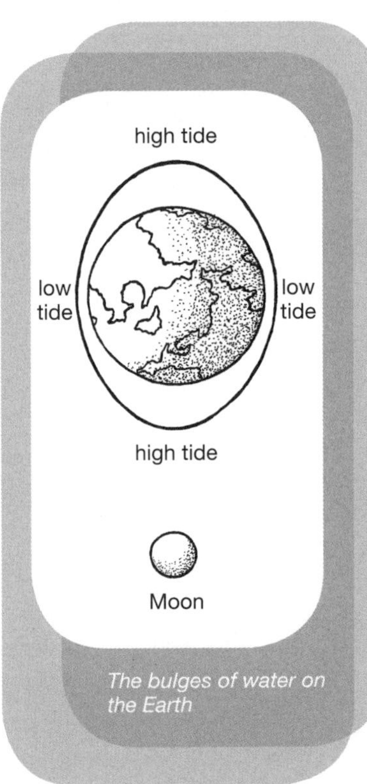

The bulges of water on the Earth

High tides The Moon's gravity causes a bulge of water on the side of the Earth closest to the Moon and another on the opposite side of the Earth.

Low tides In between the bulges there is a lot less water and tide is low.

Spring tides These are extra large tides that occur twice a month when the Sun, Moon and Earth are lined up. The pull on the oceans due to gravity is stronger then.

Neap tides **Neap tides** are small tides that occur twice a month when the Sun, Moon and Earth are at right angles to one another. The gravity of the Sun and Moon cancel each other out, so the pull on the oceans is weaker.

Tide charts are printed regularly in the newspapers and special books, and are very useful for fishermen and sailors. The chart gives the time of high and low tide, and the height of the water in metres for different places.

For you to try

1 **Investigation: The phases of the Moon**

- **a** Collect a pressure lamp or electric lamp and a large ball or balloon as a model of the Moon.
- **b** Make the room as dark as possible and put the lamp on a chair or stool in the middle of the room to represent the Sun.
- **c** One student should act as the Earth, and another should hold the Moon and move in a circle around the Earth, as shown in the diagram below.
- **d** The student who is acting as the Earth should observe the part of the Moon that is in light and the part that is in shadow.
- **e** Also observe what happens when the Moon is between the Earth and the Sun and when the Earth is between the Moon and the Sun.
- **f** Different students should take it in turns to be the Earth and the Moon.
- **g** From your observations, draw the phases of the Moon from a new moon to a full moon and to the next new moon on a sheet of paper. Include the positions of the Earth, Moon and Sun.
- **h** What is the difference between a new moon and a full moon?
- **i** What is the order of positions of the Earth, Sun and Moon when it is full moon?
- **j** What is the order of positions of the Earth, Sun and Moon when it is new moon?

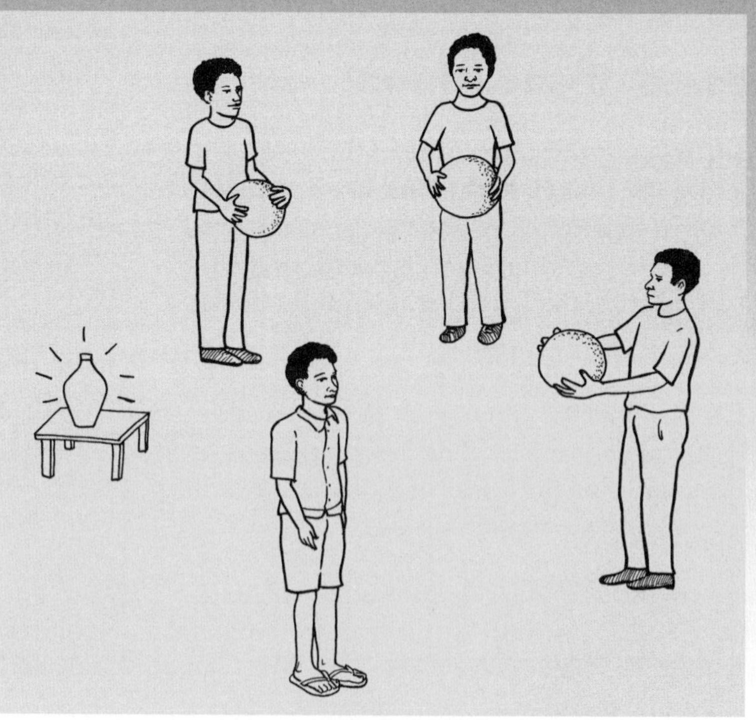

Solar and lunar eclipses

A shadow is produced when light is prevented from reaching a surface by an object. For example, when you are out in the sun your body casts a shadow on the ground. The Sun is so big that it acts like two sources of light and sometimes there will be two shadows. Where the shadows overlap there will be a full shadow which is the darkest part. Outside the full shadow there will be a lighter or partial shadow.

An **eclipse** occurs when the Earth or Moon moves into a shadow and appears dark instead of being lit by the Sun.

Solar eclipse

A **solar eclipse** is an eclipse of the Sun and can only be seen in the day time. An eclipse of the Sun occurs when the Moon comes between the Sun and the Earth so that parts of the Earth are in the Moon's shadow

A total solar eclipse occurs when a section of the Earth is in the full shadow and the sky becomes totally dark. This can be seen only from a small part of the Earth in a band about 250 km wide. Outside this band, people will see a partial solar eclipse, where only part of the Sun is covered. The sky does not become completely dark because that part of the Earth is only in the partial shadow.

In June 1983, there was an eclipse of the Sun in Papua New Guinea. There was a total eclipse in parts of Western, Central and Milne Bay provinces. People in other parts of the country had a partial eclipse.

A small part of the coast of Central Province had another total eclipse in November 1984, while other places had a partial eclipse. As far as we know, two total eclipses have never before occurred in the same place in such a short space of time.

It is dangerous to look at the Sun even during an eclipse, because it will damage your eyes.

Lunar eclipse

A **lunar eclipse** is an eclipse of the Moon and can only happen at full moon, when the Moon is in line with the Earth. The shadow of the Earth moves across the Moon so the Moon appears darker. When the Moon moves into the full

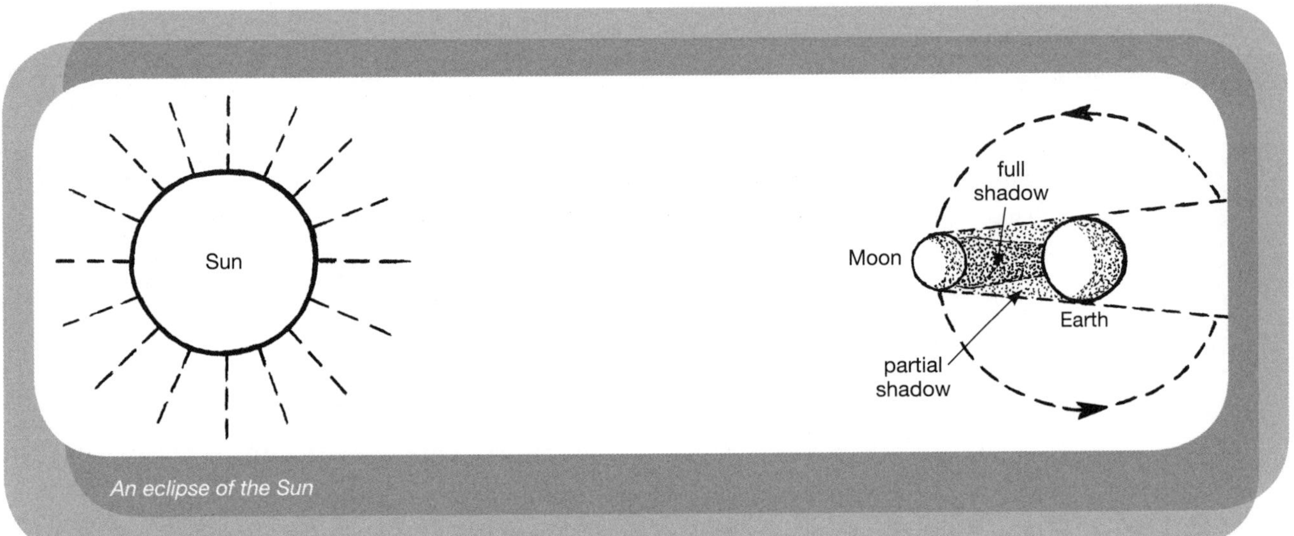

An eclipse of the Sun

shadow there is a total lunar eclipse and when the Moon is in the lighter shadow there is a partial lunar eclipse. Lunar eclipses usually happen once or twice a year. They can easily be seen, but only from the half of the Earth that is in darkness because it is night.

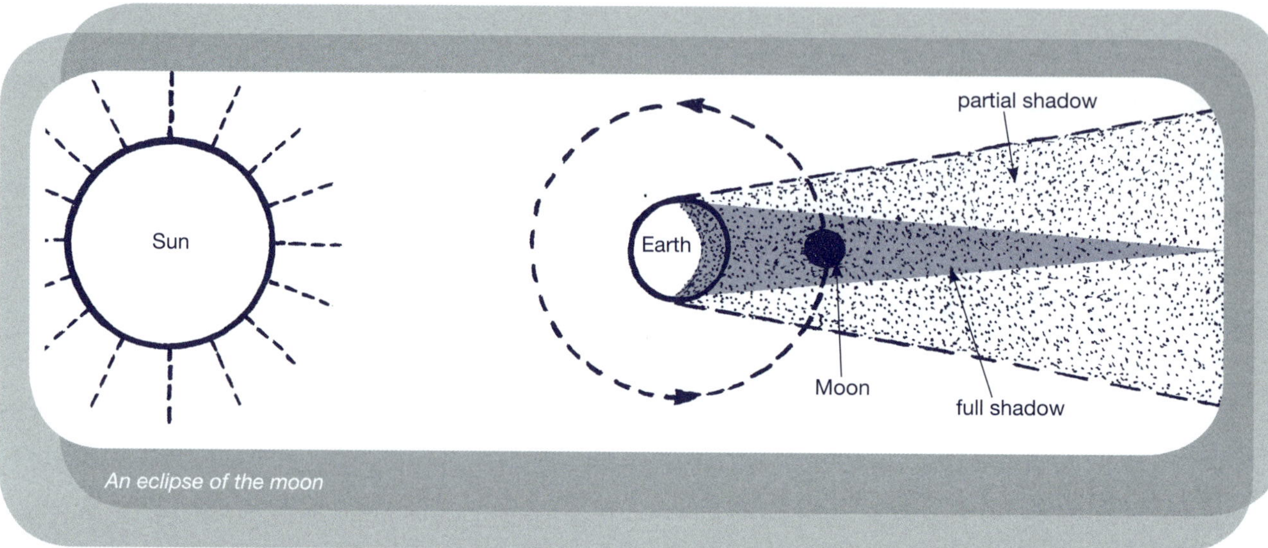

An eclipse of the moon

For you to try

1 Try to find someone who remembers the total eclipse in 1983 or 1984. Interview them or get them to answer some questions about the eclipse. Find out how long the eclipse lasted, how did people react, and how did animals and plants respond?

2 How long does it take for the Moon to rotate and orbit the Earth?

3 Make a poster to explain the high tides and low tides, spring tides and neap tides.

4 How do the phases of the Moon affect people and other living things on the Earth?

Projects

1 **Make a fossil collection**

If you live in an area where there are fossils or you can get help from someone living in such an area:

a Collect samples of rock containing fossils from your area and other areas.

b Label the fossils to show where they came from, the date and name of the fossil.

c Display your fossils for others to see.

2 Make a sundial

The sundial uses a shadow to show the time of the day. The most common sundial consists of a flat plate that has numbers for hours of the day written on it. The shadow stick, which is called a gnomon (pronounced 'no-mon'), casts a shadow on the plate. The time of the day is shown by the number that is closest to the edge of the shadow.

a Collect some cardboard, glue, scissors and a copy of the sundial template from your teacher.

b Glue the template onto the cardboard to make the base plate of your sundial.

c Cut out the shadow stick or gnomon and glue it onto a piece of cardboard.

d Place your sundial outside on flat ground in a sunny position pointing north-south, as shown in the diagram.

e Observe where the shadow of the gnomon falls at 10 am, 12 noon and 2 pm. Draw the shadow showing the shadow at these times.

f Try using your sundial to tell the time at different times of the year. Does this make any difference?

Summary questions

1 Which of the following statements are true?

I The first rocks on Earth were sedimentary rocks.

II Molten rock or magma cools down to form sedimentary rock.

III Sedimentary rock often has layers.

A I only

B II only

C III only

D I, II and III

2 Which of the following best describes the order of events in the formation of sedimentary rocks?

I Over thousands of years sediments on the sea floor can build up and change into sedimentary rocks.

II Small pieces of clay, silt and fine sand are worn away from the rocks and carried by rivers into the sea.

III When the river reaches the sea or lake the water slows down and the sediment falls to the sea floor.

A I, II, III

B II, I, III

C II, III, I

D III, II, I

3 Which of the following statements about fossils are true and which are false?

Statement	T or F?
Fossils are the remains or evidence of living things that have been preserved.	
Fossils are only found in rock.	
Fossils can be formed in several ways.	
Fossils will form only under special conditions.	
Fossils can be found in igneous rock.	
Fossils are very common because most of the animals that lived in the past have formed fossils.	
Sedimentary rocks usually must be lifted up and then weathered before fossils can be found.	

4 Which of the following best describes the order of events in the rock cycle?

A weathering, erosion, transportation, sedimentation, uplift

B weathering, uplift, erosion, transportation, sedimentation

C weathering, erosion, transportation, uplift, sedimentation

D uplift, sedimentation, transportation, erosion, weathering

5 Match the words in the table below with the best meaning or explanation:

Word	Meaning or explanation
A Length of day	I Occurs because the Earth is tilted towards the Sun
B Night	II The Earth spinning once every 24 hours
C Season	III Time taken for the Earth to orbit the Sun once
D Year	IV Occurs on the part of the Earth facing away from the Sun

6 Match the terms in the table below with the best cause or explanation:

Term	Cause or explanation
A Low tide	I An extra large tide that occurs twice a month when the Sun, Moon and Earth are in line
B High tide	II A small tide that occurs twice a month when the Sun, Moon and Earth are at right angles to one another
C Neap tide	III A decrease in sea level that occurs twice a day on opposite sides of the Earth
D Spring tide	IV An increase in sea level that occurs twice a day on the side of the Earth closest to the Moon and on the opposite side of the Earth

7 Which of the following best describes the reason why we have seasons in different parts of the world?

A The axis of the Earth is tilted towards the Sun.

B The northern hemisphere is opposite to the southern hemisphere.

C There are different temperatures and day lengths in each season.

D Spring is followed by summer, then autumn and winter.

8 Which of the following best describes the reason for an eclipse?

A The Earth rotates on its axis but the Moon does not.

B The Earth or Moon moves into a shadow and appears dark.

C The axis of the Earth is tilted and there are phases of the Moon.

D There are 13 lunar months each year but only 12 calendar months.

9 The passage below is a summary of the main ideas of this chapter. Copy and complete the passage in your book. Using the words in the list, find the words that are missing. You can use each word only once.

cycle, eroded, formed, fossils, layers, planets, position, remains, rock, sediments, seasons, Sun, tides, tilt, weathered

_______________ can be formed in different ways. For example, rock can be formed from volcanoes and from the _______________ that are carried in water and settle on the bottom of the sea, lakes and swamps. The materials that make up rock can move in a _______________. Rock can be slowly _______________ or worn away by water and wind and the small particles can be carried or _______________ by water and settle down as sediments. Over thousands of years the sediment can form _______________ of sedimentary rock.

When plants and animals die they can become buried with the sediments and form _______________. Fossils are the preserved _______________ or traces of plants and animals that lived millions of years ago. Fossils can be used to work how long ago a rock was _______________ and what plants and animals were living at that time.

Our solar system consists of eight _______________, together with their moons, dwarf planets, asteroids, meteors and comets. We can observe changes in the _______________ of the planets, the Moon and the Sun and these changes affect our way of life. The _______________ of the Earth towards the Sun and the movement of the Earth around the _______________ affect the length of day and night and the change of the _______________. The position of the Earth, Moon and Sun causes _______________.

Glossary

adaptation the way a living thing has changed to make it more suitable for its way of life
adolescents young people, usually teenagers, who have reached puberty but are not yet adults
algae simple green plants that usually live in water or damp places e.g. seaweed
alloy a metal made by mixing two or more different metals
amber fossilised gum from a type of pine tree
amphibian an animal that is able to live on land and in water by breathing through the skin and lungs e.g. frog
amylase an enzyme that begins the chemical breakdown of starch during the process of digestion
andesite a kind of igneous rock
archaeologist people who study the past and the way that people lived by looking at the things left behind like pottery, tools etc.
asteroids lumps of rock that are found in a belt between Mars and Jupiter
astronomy the study of the planets, Sun, Moon, stars and the universe
atmosphere the layer of gases that surrounds the Earth
atmospheric pressure the weight of air pushing down on the Earth
atoms the tiny particles from which all matter is made
axis an imaginary line through the centre of the Earth
axle a rod that is connected to the centre of a wheel and that allows the wheel to turn
basalt a kind of igneous rock
bearings machine parts that make surfaces roll over each other rather than sliding over each other
Big Bang the idea or theory that the universe started with a big explosion
biodegradable materials that can rot or be broken down by decay
biology the study of living things like plants and animals
biomass the total mass of each group of organisms in a food chain
boiling the change of state that occurs when water changes into steam; the boiling point of water is 100°C
bony fish fish that have a bony skeleton and scales all over the body
brass an alloy made from copper and zinc
brittle hard but breaks easily
bronze an alloy made from copper and tin
camouflage colours and patterns that make something difficult to see
canine a pointed tooth that is used for gripping
carbohydrate a food that contains starch, sugar or cellulose
carnivore an animal that eats other animals e.g. spider
cartilaginous fish fish that have a skeleton made of cartilage or gristle e.g. shark
casting pouring liquid metal or plastic into a mould to make an object with a particular shape
cause the reasons why something happens
cells the very small building blocks from which plants and animals are made
cellulose the strong material that is found in plant cell walls
ceramics pottery that is made from clay that has been heated to a high temperature
chemical change a change that occurs to matter in which new substances are formed and energy is taken in or given out; also called a chemical reaction
chemistry the study of substances like chemicals and medicines and the way that they behave
chlorophyll the green substance found in plants that is used to make food
classification putting things into groups according to their similarities and differences
clear felling cutting down all the trees in the forest
coal a hard, black substance that is formed underground from plants and animals that lived thousands of years ago; a type of fossil fuel
comet a piece of rock and ice that orbits the Sun
community all the living things in one habitat
compound a substance that is made by joining one or two elements together
conclusion something that you decide is true because you now know that other things are true
condensation the change of state from gas to liquid
conductor something that lets heat or electricity pass through easily
conifer a plant that has exposed seeds in cones e.g. klinkii pine
consumer an animal that eats plants or other animals
control the part of an experiment in which no changes are made so that the result can be compared with the test; *see also* test
crater the round, hollow shape of the rim of a volcano or the shape left by meteorite when it hits the ground
creation story a way of explaining how something was made
crust the outer layer of the Earth

decomposer microbes such as bacteria and fungi that feed on the remains of dead plants and animals by making them rot or decompose

desalination removing salt from water by distillation

development the way in which living things grow and become bigger

digestion the breakdown of large particles of food into small, simple particles

digestive system a tube which starts at the mouth and ends at the anus that food passes through

dipstick a special metal rod that is used to measure the level of oil in an engine

distillation the process by which a liquid evaporates to a gas and then condenses back to a liquid; distillation can be used to separate substances; *see also* desalination

diverse a natural environment that contains many different types of living things

ductile can be pulled or stretched into wire

ear drum a thin piece of skin inside the ear that can detect vibrations

eclipse a shadow that hides part of the Sun or Moon

ecology the study of the relationships and interactions between living things and their surroundings

ecosystem a community and its environment

effect something that happens as a result of something else

elastic something which can stretch when a force is used and then return to its original shape and size

element the simplest kind of matter that can exist on its own e.g. copper, gold, oxygen

elimination passing faeces or undigested food out of the anus

energy energy is the ability to do work; there are different types of energy

enzyme a substance produced by a living organism that helps a chemical reaction to occur more easily

erosion small pieces of weathered rock and soil that are carried away by water and wind

evaporation the change of state from liquid to gas; a method used to separate a soluble solid from a solution

faeces undigested food that passes out of the anus

fair sensible, reasonable, logical

falling star *see* shooting star

fern a green plant that has no flowers but reproduces by producing spores on the underside of the fronds

fertiliser a chemical that is added to the soil to make plants grow better

flowering plant a plant that has enclosed seeds formed within a fruit that develops from a flower

food chain a feeding relationship in which one living thing feeds on another and that always begins with a plant

food web a feeding relationship which is made up of a number of food chains; *see also* food chain

force a push or a pull that usually makes something move or change direction

fossil the remains of plants or animals that lived thousands of years ago

fossil fuel coal, oil and natural gas that come from plants and animals that lived thousands of years ago

freezing the change of state from liquid to solid; the freezing point of water is 0° C; *see also* solidification

friction a force that slows things down or stops them moving; friction also allows things to grip so that they can move

fuel a substance that can be burned to give energy

fungi plants that have no chlorophyll but live on the dead remains of other plants and animals

galaxy a large group of millions of stars

gas matter that has no fixed volume and no fixed shape

gears wheels with teeth around their edges that fit into the teeth of another wheel or into the holes of a chain

geology the study of rocks and the Earth

geothermal heat from the rocks in the Earth; electricity can be made from geothermal energy

gills the organ that fish use to obtain oxygen from water

glacier a slow moving river of ice

gnomon the stick that casts a shadow on a sundial

granite a kind of igneous rock

gravity the force that pulls objects down

gullet a tube that has muscles that move food from the mouth to the stomach

habitat the place where an animal or plant lives in the environment

health the study of the reasons why we get sick and how we can get better

herbivore an animal that eats plants e.g. butterfly

humus decaying plants and animals

hypothesis a possible explanation that has not been proved

igneous rock rock formed from magma that has cooled and solidified at the Earth's surface (volcanic rock) or deep within the earth's surface (plutonic rock)

imprint an imprint or shape left behind by a plant or animal

incisor sharp-edged, chisel-like tooth at the front of the mouth used for biting off pieces of food

incline a slope

index fossil a fossil that can help to work out the age of the rock in which it is found

inertia the way in which heavy objects do not move easily or are difficult to stop when they are moving

inference a type of conclusion and possible explanation

insoluble something that does not dissolve

insulator something that stops heat or electricity passing through

intestine part of the digestive system; *see also* small intestine and large intestine

invertebrate an animal that does not have a backbone

kilojoule a unit of energy, equal to 1000 joules; the symbol for kilojoule is kJ

kinetic energy moving energy

lane the lines on a running track that show a runner where to run

large intestine part of the digestive system where water is absorbed into the bloodstream

lever a simple machine that can be used to make work easier; a lever is usually a strong, rigid bar or rod

liquid matter that has a fixed volume but no fixed shape

liverwort a simple green land plant that lives in cool, damp places

logging cutting down trees as part of the timber industry

lubricant a solid or liquid that reduces friction e.g. oil or grease

lubrication adding oil or grease so that the surfaces of moving parts slide over each other more easily

lunar eclipse an eclipse of the Moon that occurs when the shadow of the Earth moves across the Moon
lunar month the time taken for the Moon to go through one cycle of light and dark shapes and which lasts 28 days
machine something that helps to make work easier
magma molten rock inside the earth
magnet a piece of iron or steel that attracts iron or steel towards it
malleable can be hammered into shape
mammal an animal that has fur or hair on the body and two pairs of limbs; *see also* marsupial, monotreme and placental
marsupial a mammal in which the young develop in a pouch e.g. wallaby, bandicoot, possum
matter any material or substance that has mass and takes up space
mass the quantity of substance or amount of material in something
meteor pieces of matter that move around the solar system
meteorite a meteor that reaches the surface of the Earth
meteorology the study of the weather
melting the change of state from solid to liquid
metal solids that are usually hard and can be flattened into sheets and stretched into wires
metamorphic rock rock that has been changed because of high temperature and pressure; it is harder and looks different
milk teeth the first set of teeth in humans that begin to fall out at about age seven, after which the permanent teeth grow
Milky Way the galaxy with a spiral shape in which we live
mineralisation the process by which the minerals in a fossil are replaced with minerals from water and sediment so that a copy is made which looks like rock
mixture something that contains at least two separate substances
molar large tooth at the back of the mouth that is used for crushing; *see also* premolar
molten rock or metal that has been heated to a very high temperature and has become a thick sticky liquid
monotreme a mammal that lays eggs e.g. echidna, platypus
moss a simple green land plant that lives in cool, damp places
mould a shape or hole which is left by the body of an animal in mud, clay or ash; when the hole is filled it becomes a cast which has the same shape as the original animal
moult to lose the outer skin which is replaced by the new skin underneath e.g. lizards and insects
neap tide the lowest tide which occurs during the first quarter and last quarter of the Moon
non-renewable something that cannot easily be replaced
observation something that you notice using any of your senses
obsidian a hard, shiny black igneous rock that can be used to make sharp tools
omnivore an animal that eats both plants and animals e.g. pig, human being
opaque lets light through but scatters it, translucent
organ a part of the body that is made up of two or more different kinds of tissue that work together to carry out a particular job e.g. the heart
organism an animal or a plant; any living thing
particles the tiny parts or atoms from which all matter is made
pesticide a chemical that is used to kill insects and other pests
phases of the Moon different shapes of the Moon seen from the Earth
photosynthesis the process by which plants make their own food using sunlight
physical change a change that occurs to matter in which no new substances are formed
physics the study of forces and movement, energy and matter, tools and machines
placental a mammal in which the young develop inside the mother's womb before being born alive (e.g. dog, pig, human, whale)
plane a surface
planet a body that moves in orbit around the Sun; there are eight planets in our solar system
plankton tiny plants that live in water and are the producers in many food chains
population a group of animals of the same kind
potential energy stored energy
predator an animal that catches and eats other animals
premolar large tooth at the back of the mouth that is used for crushing; *see also* molar
prey the animals that predators eat
producer a plant
products things that are made from naturally occurring materials; the new substances that are formed in a chemical reaction
properties the way in which a substance or object behaves
protease an enzyme that breaks down complex protein to simple protein
pulley a simple machine that consists of a rope, chain or belt stretched over the rim of a wheel
pumice a very light igneous rock that can float on water
pure one substance that exists by itself
radiant energy energy that can travel through space and air in the form of electro-magnetic rays
rain shadow an area that receives less rain because of the way in which the wind is pushed up and over mountains which makes the rain fall in a different place
raw materials naturally occurring materials that are used to make products
reactants the original substances that are used up in a chemical reaction
reliable information that is honest and true so that we can believe it
reptiles cold-blooded animals that have a dry, scaly skin and lungs and that live mainly on the land e.g. snakes, crocodiles, turtles
resource something that can be used to meet the needs of people
respiration the process in which plants and animals get energy from food

rock cycle the processes of rock formation, uplift, weathering and erosion that occur in the Earth's crust

root the part of a flowering plant that is below the ground

rotation the spinning of the Earth on its axis

ruminant a herbivore that can chew its food several times and also has bacteria in its stomach that can help to split open plant cells during digestion

satellite something that orbits or travels around the Sun

saturated solution a solution in which no more solute will dissolve in the solvent

scavenger an animal that feeds on dead organisms

science a way of finding out and understanding the world around us

scientific method a way of working and solving problems

scientific processes the steps that we follow to find out things

scientists people who work in science

season a period of time that has characteristic weather and day length

sediment small particles of solid that settle at the bottom of a liquid

sedimentary rock rock that is formed from sediments that have been compressed

selective logging cutting down only certain types and sizes of trees

shoot the part of a flowering plant that is above the ground

shooting star a meteor that burns up as it enters the Earth's atmosphere leaving a fiery tail

skeleton the part of an animal that provides support; some animals have an internal skeleton made of bones, and some have an external skeleton, such as insects

small intestine part of the digestive system where a little mechanical breakdown of food takes place and a lot of chemical digestion

solar from the sun

solar eclipse an eclipse of the Sun that occurs when the Moon comes between the Sun and the Earth so that parts of the Earth are in the Moon's shadow

solar still a way of obtaining fresh water from salty water by using distillation and energy from the sun

solar system the Sun and the family of eight planets, moons and asteroids

solder an alloy made from lead and tin

solid matter that has a fixed volume and a fixed shape

solidification the change of state from liquid to solid; *see also* freezing

soluble able to dissolve

solute a substance that dissolves in a liquid

solution a mixture in which one substance is dissolved in another

solvent a liquid that can dissolve things e.g. water

spring tide the highest tide which usually occurs at full moon and new moon

staggered start different positions on the curved part of a running track at the beginning or a race so that all runners cover the same distance

stainless steel an alloy made from iron, chromium, manganese and nickel

state the condition of matter—whether it is a solid, liquid or gas

stem part of the shoot of a flowering plant that supports the leaves, buds, flowers and fruits

stomach the organ where mechanical digestion takes places using muscles that churn food around to break it into smaller pieces

streamlined having a smooth shape that reduces friction when something moves through water or air

strong something that resists the effects of forces

substance any material from which things are made

sundial a simple clock that uses the Sun to tell the time of day

suspension a mixture of small particles of insoluble solid and a liquid; *see also* sediment

system a group of organs and tissues that work together to carry out a particular job e.g. circulatory system

territory an area in which an animal lives and that it will guard or defend

test the part of an experiment in which changes are made so that the result can be compared with the control; *see also* control

thinning removing plants that look weak so that the remaining plants get more nutrients and grow better

tide a change in sea level that is caused by the gravitational pull of the Moon on the Earth

tissue a group of cells that are similar to each other e.g. skin tissue

traditional knowledge the understanding of processes and materials that people have used to live successfully

transparent lets light through or 'see-through'

turbulent water or air that is constantly moving and changing direction

universe the whole of space and everything in it, including all the stars and planets

uplift movements in the earth which push up the rocks to form mountains

variation differences in the equivalent structures of a group of living things, such as roots

vegan a person who does not eat meat or fish, or any animal products such as milk, butter or cheese

vegetarian a person who does not eat meat or fish

vertebrate an animal that has a backbone

vibration fast movement backwards and forwards

weathering the slow breaking down of rock into smaller pieces

webbed feet having skin between the toes

weight the downward pull of the Earth's gravity on the mass of an object